BEACON
BIBLE
EXPOSITIONS

BEACON BIBLE EXPOSITIONS

1. Matthew
2. Mark
3. Luke
*4. John
5. Acts
6. Romans
7. Corinthians
8. Galatians, Ephesians
9. Philippians, Colossians, Philemon
10. Thessalonians, Timothy, Titus
11. Hebrews, James, Peter
12. John, Jude, Revelation

BEACON BIBLE EXPOSITIONS

VOLUME **4**

JOHN

by

SAMUEL YOUNG

Editors
WILLIAM M. GREATHOUSE
WILLARD H. TAYLOR

BEACON HILL PRESS OF KANSAS CITY
Kansas City, Missouri

Library of Congress Catalog Card No. 74-78052

ISBN: 0-8341-0315-X

Printed in the United States of America

Permission to quote from the following copyrighted versions of the Bible is acknowledged with appreciation:

The *New English Bible* (NEB), © The Delegates of the Oxford University Press and The Syndics of the Cambridge University Press, 1961, 1970.

The *Revised Standard Version of the Bible* (RSV), copyrighted 1946, 1952, © 1971, 1973.

The *New Testament in Modern English* (Phillips), Revised Edition © by J. B. Phillips, 1958, 1960, 1972, By permission of The Macmillan Publishing Co., Inc.

The Holy Bible, New International Version (NIV), © 1978 by the New York International Bible Society.

Contents

Editors' Preface	7
Introduction to the Gospel of John	9
Topical and Situation Outline of John	13
Prologue	15
First Year of Ministry: "Signs" and Encounters	21
Central Period of Ministry	52
The Shadows Lengthen	96
Final Discourses and Events	105
Jesus' Arrest, Trial, and Execution	141
The Resurrection	160
Appendix (Sermon Outlines)	179
Reference Notes	190
Bibliography	195

Editors' Preface

No Christian preacher or teacher has been more aware of the creating and sustaining power of the Word of God than the Apostle Paul. As a stratagem in his missionary endeavors, he sought out synagogues in the major cities where he knew Jews would gather to hear the Old Testament. No doubt he calculated that he would be invited to expound the Scriptures, and so he would have a golden opportunity to preach Christ. That peripatetic preacher was confident that valid Christian experience and living could not be enjoyed apart from the Word of God, whether preached or written. To the Thessalonians he wrote: "And we also thank God constantly for this, that when you received the word of God which you heard from us, you accepted it not as the word of men but as what it really is, the word of God, which is at work in you believers" (1 Thess. 2:13, RSV). Strong Christians—and more broadly, strong churches—are born of, and nurtured on, authentic and winsome exposition of the Bible.

Beacon Bible Expositions provide a systematic, devotional Bible study program for laymen and a fresh, homiletical resource for preachers. All the benefits of the best biblical scholarship are found in them, but nontechnical language is used in the composition. A determined effort is made to relate the clarified truth to life today. The writers, Wesleyan in theological perspective, seek to interpret the gospel, pointing to the Living Word, Christ, who is the primary Subject of all scripture, the Mediator of redemption, and the Norm of Christian living.

The publication of this series is a prayerful invitation to both laymen and ministers to set out on a lifelong, systematic study of the Bible. Hopefully these studies will supply the initial impetus.

—WILLIAM M. GREATHOUSE AND
WILLARD H. TAYLOR, *Editors*

Introduction to the
Gospel of John

Significance

The Gospel of John has had a large place in the hearts of all true believers for many years. In recent days, we have observed that Dr. Billy Graham, the international evangelist, frequently recommends the Gospel of John as a good beginning place for the new or young Christian in learning to read the Scriptures for the first time.

All who write and teach and study in the area of personal devotions often speak in the superlative degree concerning this Gospel. One writer calls it "The Universal Gospel." Another identifies it as "The Gospel of Belief." Many have expressed a special love for John's Gospel, and an extra large company have witnessed that "they feel at home" in its pages.

The book carries something of the poetry of the Psalms and Hebrews. But its theology seems well advanced for its day, and it fits all generations. Jerome wrote unhesitantly, "John excels in the depth of the divine mysteries." Augustine wrote in his day, "John . . . soars like an eagle above the clouds of human infinity, and gazes upon the light of unchangeable truth with those keenest and steadiest eyes of the heart."

Martin Luther pored over its pages and preached scores of sermons out of its riches. He places it on a high plane—on a level with the book of Romans—in prime importance. He wrote emphatically, "This is the unique, tender, genuine chief Gospel. . . . Should a tyrant succeed in destroying the Holy Scriptures, and only a single copy of the Epistle to the Romans and the Gospel according to John escape him, Christianity would be saved."

Its familiar John 3:16-17 reads like the whole gospel in quick summary. Its penetration and its "unspeakable gift" portrayed puts a song in many hearts. We learned such a song as a boy in Glasgow, Scotland, many years ago. It is still true.

I am so glad that our Father in heaven
Tells of His love in the Book He has given.
Wonderful things in the Bible I see:
This is the dearest, that Jesus loves me.

John tells us that story!

A Supplement to the Synoptics

It is a bit difficult to fit the Gospel of John into the narrative style and approach of the Synoptics (Matthew, Mark, and Luke). But John's record supplements them in good order.

The writer has been greatly helped in his recent study of John by the use of *The Johannine Synopsis of the Gospels,* written by H. F. D. Sparks, Oriel Professor of the Interpretation of Holy Scripture in the University of Oxford, and published by Harper and Row in 1974. As we studied John again for ourselves, we had the feeling on numerous occasions that John may have had one or more of the Synoptists' writings before him as he wrote this Gospel. At least he seemed familiar with them so that he could supply a needed supplement and afford some reinforcement to the Christian faith.

The omissions of John are rather noticeable. Here are some apparent ones:

1. He gives no account of Jesus' birth or genealogy.
2. He does not record Jesus' baptism.
3. He makes no mention of the institution of the Lord's Supper, as such.
4. He does not record the ascension of our Lord.
5. He fails to list or discuss the usual parables.

But the inclusions or supplements that John affords are equally significant:

1. John's chronology affords us a fairly accurate ac-

count (time-wise) of Jesus' total ministry. The Synoptists do not.

2. John alone gives us the miracle of "Turning Water into Wine" at Cana.

3. His person-to-person interview with Nicodemus on the new birth has no parallel.

4. Another unprecedented person-to-person interview Jesus held with the Samaritan woman by Jacob's well.

5. John alone gives us the story of "The Raising of Lazarus from the Dead."

6. John is unique in his seven great "I Am"s.

7. John's identification of seven miracles as "signs" is not duplicated by another Gospel writer.

Authorship

In *Beacon Bible Commentary* on "The Gospel According to John," J. H. Mayfield concludes that "both internal and external evidence quite consistently point to the date of writing to around A.D. 95."[1]

Lightfoot in his discussion of the origins of John's Gospel has observed, "There is now evidence available from papyrus texts discovered in Egypt that St. John's Gospel may have been in existence soon after, if not before, A.D. 100."[2]

Hobbs, in *The Gospel of John* (1968), suggests an estimated date of writing between A.D. 80 and 90. He also quotes Hobbs's summary that "by the last quarter of the second century, the Fourth Gospel was accepted by the Church as the canonical work of the Apostle John."[3]

Boice, in his first volume of *The Gospel of John* (1975), observes that the more recent papyrus discoveries "have tended to push back the date" for the writing of John's Gospel. He notes, "Now some are ready to acknowledge a date within 30 or 40 years of Christ's death."[4] He reminds us that archaeologists have found "pieces of papyrus of John's Gospel (probably) discarded about A.D. 125."

All of this would suggest to us a date earlier than A.D. 95.

Some scholars have been troubled by the writer's use of the Logos idea as well as the frequent use of terms such as, "light and darkness, life and death." These studies have tended to trace the use of such terms to the influence of Greek thought on the Christian Church—and such influence has usually been timed much later than the first century. However, As Boice observes, Qumran, where the Dead Sea scrolls were discovered, is located not far from Jerusalem in "the very area where John placed the earliest events of Christ's ministry."[5] The literature these scrolls contained "revealed the same use of the so-called Greek terms . . . as found in John's Gospel."

A few have chided John because he did not name or identify himself specifically within his Gospel. However, he does call himself "the disciple whom Jesus loved." It is also interesting to us that John does not even name his own elder brother, James, even although both brothers were in our Savior's inner circle of the apostles. Could it be that the Sons of Thunder, and their ambitious mother, had captured something of Jesus' view of service, and now it shows through by John's silence in places?

But as we ponder again the grip and charm of this Gospel, we gather a feeling of reassurance and the ring of divine authority. Here is an "insider" writing out of his own knowledge and experience, with clarity and penetration. Also, there has come the perspective of the years that what was spoken in earlier years by way of promise has been fulfilled in fact among the body of believers. This author writes as an eyewitness and he wanted others to learn the truth that was eternal and that is received only through faith.

Even in his Prologue John reports, "The Word was made flesh, and dwelt among us." Then he adds personally, "And we saw his glory, such glory as befits the Father's only Son, full of grace and truth" (John 1:14, NEB).

Topical and Situation Outline

Prologue (1:1-18)

First Year of Ministry: "Signs" and Encounters
    John the Baptist's Witness (1:19-34)
    The First Disciples (1:35-51)
    ✳ The Marriage Feast at Cana: The First Sign (2:1-11)
    The Cleansing of the Temple (2:13-22)
    In Capernaum and Jerusalem (2:12, 23-25)
    Encounter with Nicodemus (3:1-21)
    John Again Bears Witness to Jesus (3:22-36)
    A Samaritan Woman in Need (4:1-42)
    ✴ Healing of the Nobleman's Son: The Second Sign (4:43-54)
    ✴ Healing the Derelict: The Third Sign (5:1-18)
    A Discourse of Jesus: A Response (5:19-47)

Central Period of Ministry
    ✴ Feeding of the Five Thousand: The Fourth Sign (6:1-14)
    ✴ Jesus Walks on the Water: The Fifth Sign (6:15-21)
    Discourse on Jesus the Bread of Life (6:22-59)
    Some Disciples Hesitate; Others Go Back (6:60-71)
    Jesus Hides Out in Galilee (7:1-9)
    The Feast of Tabernacles; Controversy (7:10-36, 45-52)
    Promise of the Holy Spirit's Coming (7:37-44)
    The Woman Taken in Adultery (8:1-11)
    Jesus the Light of the World (8:12-20)
    Further Teaching of Jesus About Who He Is (8:21-59)
    ✴ A Blind Beggar Receives His Sight: The Sixth Sign (9:1-41)
    A Parable of the Shepherd (10:1-21)
    At the Feast of Dedication (10:22-42)
    ✴ The Raising of Lazarus: The Seventh Sign (11:1-53)
    Jesus Withdraws to Ephraim (11:54-57)

The Shadows Lengthen
    The Supper and Anointing at Bethany (12:1-11)
    The Messianic Triumphal Entry (12:12-19)
    The Greeks Inquire for Jesus; Jesus Again Withdraws
        (12:20-43)
    Jesus, the Father's Own Agent (12:44-50)

Final Discourses and Events
    Upper Room Ministry and Example (13:1-20)
    The Prophecy of Betrayal (13:21-30)
    A New Commandment of Love (13:31-35)
    The Prophecy of Peter's Denial (13:36-38)
    Strength and Guidance Promised Through the Holy Spirit
        (14:1-31)
    Jesus the True Vine (15:1-27)
    The Holy Spirit to Become Permanent Teacher (16:1-33)
    The High Priestly Prayer (17:1-26)

Jesus' Arrest, Trial, and Execution
    Jesus' Surrender in the Garden (18:1-11)
    Trial Before Annas (Ecclesiastical) (18:12-14, 19-24)
    Peter's Denial (18:15-18, 25-27)
    Trial Before Pilate (Political) (18:28—19:16)
    The Crucifixion (19:17-37)
    His Burial (19:38-42)

The Resurrection
    The Empty Tomb (20:1-10)
    The Appearance to Mary Magdalene (20:11-18)
    First Appearance to the Disciples; Thomas Doubts
        (20:19-25)
    Second Appearance to the Disciples; Thomas Believes
        (20:26-29)
    Motive for Writing the Gospel (20:30-31)
    The Final Appearance in Galilee (21:1-14)
    The Commission to Peter and to John (21:15-23)
    Concluding Notes (21:24-25)

Prologue

John 1:1-18

JOHN **1**

_____

The Incarnate God

John 1:1-18

1 In the beginning was the Word, and the Word was with God, and the Word was God.

2 The same was in the beginning with God.

3 All things were made by him; and without him was not any thing made that was made.

4 In him was life; and the life was the light of men.

5 And the light shineth in darkness; and the darkness comprehended it not.

6 There was a man sent from God, whose name was John.

7 The same came for a witness, to bear witness of the Light, that all men through him might believe.

8 He was not that Light, but was sent to bear witness of that Light.

9 That was the true Light, which lighteth every man that cometh into the world.

10 He was in the world, and the world was made by him, and the world knew him not.

11 He came unto his own, and his own received him not.

12 But as many as received him, to them gave he power to become the sons of God, even to them that believe on his name:

13 Which were born, not of blood, nor of the will of the flesh, nor of the will of man, but of God.

14 And the Word was made flesh, and dwelt among us, (and we beheld his glory, the glory as of the only begotten of the Father,) full of grace and truth.

15 John bare witness of him, and cried, saying, This was he of whom I spake, He that cometh after me is preferred before me: for he was before me.

16 And of his fulness have all we received, and grace for grace.

17 For the law was given by Moses, but grace and truth came by Jesus Christ.

18 No man hath seen God at any time; the only begotten Son, which is in the bosom of the Father, he hath declared him.

In our introduction we pointed out that new and young Christians are sometimes directed to the Gospel of

John as a good place to begin to read and study the Bible. But John's opening lines almost "choke" the young Christian at first. They are majestic, but they seem baffling for beginners.

We must confess that the apostle here is not writing with a fine quill. He is using a brush as an artist would in painting a portrait. But these are not the abstractions of a closet-room philosopher whose every sentence requires a completely new vocabulary in order to know what he is talking about. G. Campbell Morgan has warned us that this prologue is not simply a preface, in the usual sense of introduction. He writes, "The whole truth, as John saw it, concerning 'Jesus Christ the Son of God' is found in these first eighteen verses."[1]

1. The Old Testament begins with, "In the beginning God created the heavens and the earth" (Gen. 1:1). John's gospel begins with, "In the beginning was the Word, and the Word was with God, and the Word was God" (1:1). In John Wesley's own translation the first line reads, "In the beginning *existed* the Word." He explains in his notes, "In the beginning of heaven and earth, and this whole frame of created beings, the Word existed without any beginning." The Psalmist had also written concerning creation, "The Lord's word made the heavens, all the host of heaven was made at his command" (Ps. 33:6, NEB).

John uses "logos" to mean Word in two verses, 1 and 14. Westcott in his notes is careful to point out that "the term [logos] never has the sense of *reason* in the New Testament," and that "St. John introduces the term without explanation. He assumes that his readers are familiar with it."

2. Westcott suggests John's three clauses relate to the Word: *(a)* in relation to time; *(b)* mode (or manner) of being; and *(c)* His character. He summarizes: "These three clauses answer to the three great moments of the Incarnation of the Word declared in verse 14. He who 'was God,' became flesh: He who 'was with God,' tabernacled

among us: He who 'was in the beginning,' became (in time)."[2]

This incarnation was God's message of revelation of himself. Morgan states it tersely, "Jesus is the Exegesis of God."[3] This is what Jesus was saying to Philip (whom he had taught personally for about three years): "Have I been all this time with you, Philip, and still do you not know me? Anyone who has seen me has seen the Father. Then how can you say, 'Show us the Father?'" (John 14:9, NEB).

3. It was only in the Incarnation (when the Word became flesh) that Jesus' life became the light of men. The Word is not an impersonal principle, revealing the light of truth —bright and penetrating. The Word became personal to humanity when He became man. Jesus' favorite name for himself was Son of Man. He needed to become man to afford us Redemption in the economy of grace, but we also needed Him as man in the clear revelation of God himself. What a summary John affords us in verse four: "In him was life; and the life was the light of men"! Here the way to God is not simply a light on a faraway mountain, too distant and too steep for us to climb. It is also a life-giving strength through the Son, thus affording grace and power for our task. The darkness of sin is all around us, immediate and entrenched, John seems to say. But His light shines through to us.

A Christian missionary to Japan, who had to return home during World War II because of the conflict, felt dismayed as she approached the New York Harbor. Then it came to her as a whisper from above, "All the darkness of the world cannot put out the light of a single candle!" It gave her the "lift" she needed, so she brushed back her tears while she promised God she would pray and wait for another day. Actually, the message of verse five is stronger than the burning candle. The light is Jesus Christ. His light was lit on Calvary's brow and it shines on because the message of the open tomb is that "He is alive forevermore." The Holy Spirit himself fans the flame of truth and illuminates our way. We like the NEB translation here of verse five: "The light shines on in the dark, and the darkness has never quenched it."

Jowett makes the radiance of Jesus' light sing with the rhythm of truth and the cadence of joy. "He [Jesus] lit up sin and showed its true color! He lit up sorrow and transfigured it! He lit up duty and gave it a new face. He lit up common work, and glorified it. He lit up death, and we could see through it! But above all, He lit up God, and 'the people that sat in darkness saw a great light.'"[4]

In the prologue the writer soon introduces John the Baptist as a witness to the light. However, he summarizes the Baptist's mission, "That all men might believe through him" (7).

4. Here at the outset the writer anticipates future outcome and confesses, "He came to his own home, and his own people received him not. But to all who received him, who believed on his name, he gave power to become children of God" (11-12, RSV). The NEB translates it, "Unto them he gave the right to become children of God." In his own translation, John Wesley puts it, "To them gave he privilege to become sons of God."

The Incarnation is stated in terse but resplendent summary: "So the Word became flesh; he came to dwell among us, and we saw his glory, such glory as befits the Father's only Son, full of grace and truth" (14, NEB). John the Apostle may be referring here to the Mount of Transfiguration scene reported by both Matthew and Mark in their respective accounts of the gospel. However, it should be noted that when they came down from that peak of revelation, Jesus himself admonished His inner circle, "Tell the vision to no man, until the Son of man be risen from the dead" (Matt. 17:9).

But the ultimate glory that Jesus prayed for in the 17th chapter of John was to be realized on Calvary. Boice points out that through the Incarnation "God sanctified the value of human life." However, he cautions us that the Incarnation is but "the second greatest truth in the Bible." He insists, "The greatest is that this God who became man could also love us enough to go to the cross and die for us personally."[5]

Archbishop Temple also insists that the Incarnation itself is not the final word. He reasons, "For the sacrifice and the humiliation are the divine glory. If God is love, His glory most of all shines forth in whatever most fully expresses love. The cross of shame is the theme of glory."[6]

5. In John's burst of praise at the climax of the Prologue he declares, "From his fulness have we all received and grace upon grace. For the law was given through Moses; grace and truth came through Jesus Christ" (16-17, RSV). Phillips paraphrases "grace upon grace" to read, "There is grace in our lives because of his grace."

It is rather significant to note here that once John the Apostle names Jesus Christ in verse 17, he *never again* identifies Him in his Gospel as "the Word"!

In these final verses (16-18), Jesus is depicted as the perfect balance between grace and truth; not grace alone in the sense of mercy and compassion, or love alone to the neglect of truth and righteousness. However, truth is not abstract, neither does it stand alone. It is cradled in God's holy love, the prime and moving cause for God's redeeming grace. Conversely, this grace is not mercy and compassion winking at the purity of God's holiness. Hence Calvary.

Charles Wesley's 18th-century hymn still sings in our hearts today. It centers in Jesus Christ as Savior and Lord.

> *Other refuge have I none;*
>   *Hangs my helpless soul on Thee.*
> *Leave, ah, leave me not alone;*
>   *Still support and comfort me!*
> *All my trust on Thee is stayed,*
>   *All my help from Thee I bring;*
> *Cover my defenseless head*
>   *With the shadow of Thy wing.*

Thou, O Christ, art all I want;
More than all in Thee I find.
Raise the fallen, cheer the faint,
Heal the sick, and lead the blind.
Just and holy is Thy name;
I am all unrighteousness.
False and full of sin I am;
Thou art full of truth and grace.

First Year of Ministry: "Signs" and Encounters

John 1:19—5:47

John the Baptist's Witness

John 1:19-34

19 And this is the record of John, when the Jews sent priests and Levites from Jerusalem to ask him, Who art thou?
20 And he confessed, and denied not; but confessed, I am not the Christ.
21 And they asked him, What then? Art thou Elias? And he saith, I am not. Art thou that prophet? And he answered, No.
22 Then said they unto him, Who art thou? that we may give an answer to them that sent us. What sayest thou of thyself?
23 He said, I am the voice of one crying in the wilderness, Make straight the way of the Lord, as said the prophet Esaias.
24 And they which were sent were of the Pharisees.
25 And they asked him, and said unto him, Why baptizest thou then, if thou be not that Christ, nor Elias, neither that prophet?
26 John answered them, saying, I baptize with water: but there standeth one among you, whom ye know not;
27 He it is, who coming after me is preferred before me, whose shoe's latchet I am not worthy to unloose.
28 These things were done in Bethabara beyond Jordan, where John was baptizing.
29 The next day John seeth Jesus coming unto him, and saith, Behold the Lamb of God, which taketh away the sin of the world.
30 This is he of whom I said, After me cometh a man which is preferred before me: for he was before me.
31 And I knew him not: but that he should be made manifest to Israel, therefore am I come baptizing with water.
32 And John bare record, saying, I saw the Spirit descending from heaven like a dove, and it abode upon him.
33 And I knew him not: but he that sent me to baptize with water, the same said unto me, Upon whom thou shalt see the Spirit descending, and remaining on him, the same is he which baptizeth with the Holy Ghost.
34 And I saw, and bare record that this is the Son of God.

John the Baptist's witness concerning Jesus was given to a deputation of priests and Levites sent to inquire who he (the Baptist) was. The latter readily answered No to their three specific questions, namely that he was not the Christ (the Messiah), nor the Elijah (to come), nor the prophet of an undesignated mission. Then they asked specifically, "Who are you?" John answered in the language of Isaiah, "I am the voice of one crying in the wilderness, 'Make straight the way of the Lord'" (23, RSV). At least, John was a voice and not an echo.

1. Immediately some of the investigating committee probed the Baptist further by asking, "Why then are you baptizing?" John answered, "I baptize with water, but among you stands one whom you know not, even he who comes after me, the thong of whose sandal I am not worthy to untie!" (26-27, RSV). The apostle explains that all of this took place in Bethany, beyond the Jordan, where John was baptizing.

It is also interesting to note here in passing that this mission sent from Jerusalem is not mentioned by the Synoptists. But the next day John the Baptist seized a climactic moment, as he saw Jesus coming toward him. "'Look,' he said, 'There is the Lamb of God; it is he who takes away the sin of the world. This is he of whom I spoke when I said, "After me a man is coming who takes rank before me"; for before I was born, he already was'" (29-30, NEB). The Baptist then confesses freely that he himself did not know the Christ until the Spirit identified Him by coming down on Him like a dove and remaining on Him. He further explained, this was the real reason he (John) baptized with water, namely, "that he (the Messiah) might be revealed to Israel" (31, RSV). John further asserts that this was the One who would baptize with the Holy Spirit. Then the Baptist lays it on the line: "And I have seen and borne witness that this is the Son of God" (34, RSV).

In the prologue, John the Apostle had said that there was one sent to bear witness to the light. He existed for that mission; it was his *raison d'etre* (reason for being)— the real justification for his new mode of existence. Now the Baptist confirms this mission with his own public witness (31*b*).

2. How fitting that John the Baptist should identify Jesus as "The Lamb of God," as Temple points out: "The *Lamb of God* is the victim whom God provides, as He provided the ram in the place of Isaac (Genesis 22:8); and this Lamb Himself *beareth away the sin of the world*. In the coming of Christ, God himself is active; He provides (for indeed He himself is) the offering, and He himself makes it."[1] The Baptist not only identifies Jesus, he delineates His mission. This Messiah was no swashbuckling commander that came to rid Israel of her enemies; He came to deliver them from their own sin and rebellion and He did it God's way. It was love and not might that would redeem. It was the Lamb that would reign, and His was the Kingdom that would never end.

3. John the Baptist stands as a transition messenger or prophet of God before the inauguration of Jesus' ministry and mission. The fearless ministry of the Baptist captured the attention of Jesus, and John's self-effacing strength could not be forgotten. Jesus' tribute to him is a penetrating classic concerning this servant of God. Both Matthew and Luke record Jesus' tribute, given even when the Baptist John was wavering a bit as he languished in jail. After the Baptist's messengers left to give Jesus' reply to him, Jesus paid tribute to John before the people! "What did you go out in the wilderness to behold? A reed shaken with the wind? What then did you go out to see? A man clothed in soft raiment? Behold, those who are gorgeously appareled and live in luxury are in kings' courts. What then did you go out to see? A prophet? Yes, I tell you, and more than a prophet" (Luke 7:24*b*-26, RSV). What a crescendo!

    (1) A reed shaken with the wind?
    (2) A man in soft clothes?
    (3) A prophet?
    (4) More than a prophet
    (5) None is greater than John!

Actually, John the Baptist introduced Jesus to the religious community of Israel as "The Lamb of God who takes away the sin of the world" (29). He concludes by declaring unequivocably, "He is the Son of God" (34).

The First Disciples

John 1:35-51

35 Again the next day after John stood, and two of his disciples;
36 And looking upon Jesus as he walked, he saith, Behold the Lamb of God!
37 And the two disciples heard him speak, and they followed Jesus.
38 Then Jesus turned, and saw them following, and saith unto them, What seek ye? They said unto him, Rabbi, (which is to say, being interpreted, Master,) where dwellest thou?
39 He saith unto them, Come and see. They came and saw where he dwelt, and abode with him that day: for it was about the tenth hour.
40 One of the two which heard John speak, and followed him, was Andrew, Simon Peter's brother.
41 He first findeth his own brother Simon, and saith unto him, We have found the Messias, which is, being interpreted, the Christ.
42 And he brought him to Jesus. And when Jesus beheld him, he said, Thou art Simon the son of Jona: thou shalt be called Cephas, which is by interpretation, A stone.
43 The day following Jesus would go forth into Galilee, and findeth Philip, and saith unto him, Follow me.
44 Now Philip was of Bethsaida, the city of Andrew and Peter.
45 Philip findeth Nathanael, and saith unto him, We have found him, of whom Moses in the law, and the prophets, did write, Jesus of Nazareth, the son of Joseph.
46 And Nathanael said unto him, Can there any good thing come out of Nazareth? Philip saith unto him, Come and see.
47 Jesus saw Nathanael coming to him, and saith of him, Behold an Israelite indeed, in whom is no guile!
48 Nathanael saith unto him, Whence knowest thou me? Jesus answered and said unto him, Before that Philip called thee, when thou wast under the fig tree, I saw thee.
49 Nathanael answered and saith unto him, Rabbi, thou art the Son of God; thou art the King of Israel.
50 Jesus answered and said unto him, Because I said unto thee, I saw thee under the fig tree, believest thou? thou shalt see greater things than these.
51 And he saith unto him, Verily, verily, I say unto you, Hereafter ye shall see heaven open, and the angels of God ascending and descending upon the Son of man.

It is easy to identify the modesty of the author of this Gospel by the name he uses for himself, "the disciple whom Jesus loved." We are inclined to read this as an "editorial *we*" that seems to him to be good taste. Robertson notes, "In the Fourth Gospel John is never visible and Jesus is never invisible."[2] Surely this is better than the reverse trend where one is more concerned with his own identity and place in history than in the one he portrays! Besides, John does not "parade" his ministry.

1. Jesus' active ministry begins about the time when John the Baptist had reached the climax of his popularity and ministry. He seemed to be "shunting" some of his own leading followers into Jesus' circle. They eventually became a part of the Master's "inner circle." The record reads, "The next day again John [the Baptist] was standing with two of his disciples when Jesus passed by. John looked towards him and said, 'There is the Lamb of God.' The two disciples heard him say this and followed Jesus" (35-37, NEB).

This was probably the last time John the Baptist saw Jesus, but what a valedictory for that last of the Old Testament prophets! One of the two involved in this transfer of allegiance was Andrew, and we are inclined to conclude that the other one was John, the writer. Jowett reports concerning this transition, "In forgetting John they found the King. They passed the signpost and arrived at home!"[3]

Promptly Andrew looked up his brother, Peter, and said, "We have found the Messiah" (which is Hebrew for Christ). Then Andrew led Peter to Jesus and the Master named him "Peter, the Rock." Next day, Jesus looked up Philip from Bethsaida and said, "Follow me," and he did. (Philip was actually the only one of the original group that Jesus recruited personally.) In turn, Philip found his friend Nathanael and reported to him, "We have found Jesus of Nazareth, of whom Moses and the prophets wrote." But Nathanael's rejoinder was, "Nazareth! Can anything good come out of Nazareth?" Philip's tactful reply was "Come and see." When he met Jesus and conversed, Nathanael "caved in" with, "Rabbi, thou art the Son of God; thou art the King of Israel" (49).

2. Now they were six in number, assuming that by now John had won over James, his elder brother. It was a case of seeking and finding, on a man-to-man basis. Jesus impressed all of them with His penetrating analysis of each man, and they were won over.

At the close, Jesus promises a ladder reaching from earth to heaven, better than Jacob's dream. It was in this instance (31) that John first employs the favorite, "Verily, verily," which he used some 18 times in this Gospel. It really means, "Amen, amen," and occurs only in the Gospel of John, and is used only by Christ himself. It reminds us of Isaiah's reference to "the God whose name is Amen" (65:16, NEB). It speaks of the reliability and assurance of God, for the name of God always describes His character. No wonder the apostle John wanted men to believe in Him!

3. The final section of this immediate passage before us closes by calling Jesus "the Son of man." Here the designation relates Him to all humanity rather than to a special people or race. No wonder John later indicates the realm of His redemption extends to "whosoever believeth in him." Such is the measure of God's redemption and grace.

Mayfield in his *commentary on John* (BBC) summarizes this chapter enumerating "eight highly descriptive titles (in it) ascribed to the Incarnate One." Here they are and be sure you read the context for yourself, if possible, in at least two different translations. John writes about Jesus: "He is Logos, the living 'Word' (1:14); 'Son of God,' very God; 'Rabbi,' the Master Teacher (38); 'Messias,' 'Christ,' the Anointed One (41); 'Jesus of Nazareth,' the God-man in history (45); King of Israel, the One crowned King by those who put their faith in Him (49); and 'the Son of man,' very man (51)."[4]

The Marriage Feast at Cana: The First Sign

John 2:1-11 ·

> 1 And the third day there was a marriage in Cana of Galilee; and the mother of Jesus was there:
> 2 And both Jesus was called, and his disciples, to the marriage.
> 3 And when they wanted wine, the mother of Jesus saith unto him, They have no wine.
> 4 Jesus saith unto her, Woman, what have I to do with thee? mine hour is not yet come.
> 5 His mother saith unto the servants, Whatsoever he saith unto you, do it.
> 6 And there were set there six waterpots of stone, after the manner of the purifying of the Jews, containing two or three firkins apiece.
> 7 Jesus saith unto them, Fill the waterpots with water. And they filled them up to the brim.
> 8 And he saith unto them, Draw out now, and bear unto the governor of the feast. And they bare it.
> 9 When the ruler of the feast had tasted the water that was made wine, and knew not whence it was: (but the servants which drew the water knew;) the governor of the feast called the bridegroom,
> 10 And saith unto him, Every man at the beginning doth set forth good wine; and when men have well drunk, then that which is worse; but thou hast kept the good wine until now.
> 11 This beginning of miracles did Jesus in Cana of Galilee, and manifested forth his glory; and his disciples believed on him.

It was at a charming wedding scene that Jesus performed His first miracle, or what John calls a "sign." His mother was present there and seemed to have a hand in the wedding. Jesus and His disciples were there. He seemed to be interested in the normal joys of life. Redding observes, "Jesus did not need a protected, monastic setting to display His power; He went where life was and hallowed any scene. He was never out of place. . . . This early glimpse at Cana shows Christ most completely at home in mixed company and loving life for all its worth."[5]

In his classical 13 discourses on the Lord's Sermon on the Mount, John Wesley discusses Jesus' words, "Ye are the salt of the earth. . . . Ye are the light of the world." He writes: "Christianity is essentially a social religion; and that to turn it into a solitary religion is indeed to destroy it." Then he adds, "I mean not only that it cannot subsist so well, but that it cannot subsist at all, without society—without living and conversing with other men."[6]

In general, Jesus did not perform His miracles for show, neither did He display them on prime time—to borrow a current radio and TV earmark—carrying political overtones.

1. In Jesus' day those wedding feasts lasted for days and perhaps a week. They ran out of wine early and Jesus' mother discovered it and reported to Him, "They have no wine left" (3b, NEB). He answered, "Woman, what have I to do with thee? Mine hour is not yet come" (4). At first glance, this looks like a "brushoff," but that doesn't sound like Jesus. Even the address, "Woman," is one of tenderness, for He uses it again in his last clear moments on the Cross when He was performing His last service of provision for her through John, the apostle. Also, the term "mine hour is not yet come" reappears numerous times throughout this Gospel and always points ultimately to the Cross. It is rather interesting that He spoke it first to His mother here and last to His Heavenly Father in John 17:1. We like these paraphrases of Jesus' reply: (a) "Your concern, mother, is not mine" (NEB), and (b) "Why do you involve me?" (NIV).

With something like a woman's hunch, His mother said to the servants, "Do whatever he tells you." What a theme that would make for a message!

2. Presently Jesus told the servants to fill six large stone jars (standing nearby) with water. Their capacity was some 20 gallons each. When they were filled to the brim He told the servants, "Now draw some off and take to the steward of the feast." He tasted the water (now turned to wine) and pronounced it the best, but he was puzzled. John observes that this sign (or miracle) led His disciples to believe in Him. Lightfoot calls the sign "a visible pointer to the invisible truth about Him," and he concludes that "the entire Gospel is a 'Book of Signs.'"[7]

The Cleansing of the Temple

John 2:13-22

> 13 And the Jews' passover was at hand, and Jesus went up to Jerusalem,
> 14 And found in the temple those that sold oxen and sheep and doves, and the changers of money sitting:
> 15 And when he had made a scourge of small cords, he drove them all out of the temple, and the sheep, and the oxen; and poured out the changers' money, and overthrew the tables;
> 16 And said unto them that sold doves, Take these things hence; make not my Father's house an house of merchandise.
> 17 And his disciples remembered that it was written, The zeal of thine house hath eaten me up.
> 18 Then answered the Jews and said unto him, What sign shewest thou unto us, seeing that thou doest these things?
> 19 Jesus answered and said unto them, Destroy this temple, and in three days I will raise it up.
> 20 Then said the Jews, Forty and six years was this temple in building, and wilt thou rear it up in three days?
> 21 But he spake of the temple of his body.
> 22 When therefore he was risen from the dead, his disciples remembered that he had said this unto them; and they believed the scripture, and the word which Jesus had said.

It is rather easy to miss some points in portraying Jesus Christ in His entirety. We learned long ago to sing:

> *Gentle Jesus, meek and mild,*
> *Look upon this little child.*

It is surely true that He is basically gentle, but He is not always meek and mild.

1. In the scene before us Jesus had gone to Jerusalem because the time of the Passover was near and this was His first visit to the Temple after His Messianic mission had begun.

Here He soon discovered certain built-in questionable practices that had been gaining strength over the years. Jesus discerned that these practices (under the cover of Temple operations) were actually a corruption of the priests' sacred trust. One item covered a coin exchange, for the Jews were not allowed to use foreign coins in paying their Temple tax—the implication was that such foreign coins would corrupt their sacred worship. Also, there was a need for the sale of animals to be offered in the Temple sacrifices, especially for those who came from faraway places. For the coin exchange there was a small fee at first, and for the animals a reasonable profit margin was allowed. In time, the profit in both areas expanded and the volume increased greatly.

Jesus read all of this as a profanity upon His Father's house and a desecration upon His name. His soul burned with an inner fire and it broke out in a blaze as He approached the Gentile court when He saw that the Gentiles were excluded by the expansive spread. By now, He had picked up some cords and made an impromptu whip out of them and with no delay, He "drove them out of the temple, sheep, cattle, and all. He upset the tables of the money-changers, scattering their coins" (15, NEB). Nothing stopped Him. "Then he turned on the dealers in pigeons: 'Take them out,' he said; 'you must not turn my Father's house into a market'" (16, NEB).

2. Sure enough, Jesus looked like an iconoclast. Years later, Peter wrote to the churches in Lesser Asia, "For the time is come that judgment must begin at the house of God" (1 Pet. 1:7)

Jesus' drama was more than a silent pantomime; it was a practical house cleaning and the chief offenders knew who they were. The Reformer had surprised them and they were "stung" by the accuracy of His quick and penetrating summary. He knew the leaders were the true insiders and big profiteers.

In turn, the Jews challenged Him with, "What sign can you show as authority for your action?" His reply was puzzling, "Destroy this temple and in three days I will raise it again." With some contempt, they replied, "It has taken forty-six years to build this temple. Are you going to raise it again in three days?" (19-20, NEB).

3. John explains that the temple Jesus was referring to was the temple of His body, and that the disciples them-

selves identified His real meaning only after His resurrection. It was ironical also that later on at His trial before the high priest, "Two men alleged that He had said, 'I can pull down the temple of God and build it in three days'" (cf. Matt. 26:60b-61). But when the high priest pressed for an answer, Jesus was silent.

Matthew records an occasion when certain scribes and Pharisees asked Him for a sign, His answer was, "An evil and adulterous generation seeks for a sign; but no sign shall be given to it except the sign of the prophet Jonah. For as Jonah was three days and three nights in the belly of the whale, so shall the Son of Man be three days and three nights in the heart of the earth" (12:38-40, RSV).

Jesus the Reformer has afforded us a good example of the price of His devotion. Here it is in outline:

(1) The Cost of Devotion—doing the Father's will, constantly.

(2) The Courage of Devotion—cleansing corruption.

(3) The Consequence (ultimate) of Devotion—the Cross.

(4) The Climax of Devotion—at home with the Father.

In Capernaum and Jerusalem

John 2:12, 23-25

> 12 After this he went down to Capernaum, he, and his mother, and his brethren, and his disciples: and they continued there not many days.

> 23 Now when he was in Jerusalem at the passover, in the feast day, many believed in his name, when they saw the miracles which he did.
> 24 But Jesus did not commit himself unto them, because he knew all men,
> 25 And needed not that any should testify of man: for he knew what was in man.

This departure down to Capernaum (verse 12) reminds us that eventually Capernaum became Jesus' headquarters and a while after this Matthew records it, "When he heard that John the Baptist had been arrested, Jesus withdrew to Galilee; and leaving Nazareth he went and settled in Capernaum on the Sea of Galilee, in the district of Zebulun and Naphtali" (12-13, NEB).

Also in the short section (verses 23-25) we have a record again of Jesus' penetrating gaze and practical demands. He knew that faith built on miracles alone would not last. Such faith demands repeated and increased miracles; meanwhile they have failed to lean on the One who is dependable. As Morgan put it, "Their faith was shallow because it was based on wonder."[8] We think it lacked an ethical tone. Jesus did not commit himself to those who did not commit themselves one by one to Him. Complete reliability is based on our utter dependence— with no reservations—on Him. In practical living, faith is interchangeable. Although God is the Giver, faith is both a gift and a decision. We must receive Him with both hands open and nothing behind our back. Our darkest sins and deepest needs are not hid from Him. When we "hedge" in our faith, there is often a sense of bluff or strut. Faith is a leap based on the reliability of Him "who sacrificed himself for us, to set us free from all wickedness and to make us a pure people, marked out for his own, and eager to do good" (Titus 2:14, NEB).

JOHN 3

Encounter with Nicodemus

John 3:1-21

1 There was a man of the Pharisees, named Nicodemus, a ruler of the Jews:
2 The same came to Jesus by night, and said unto him, Rabbi, we know that thou art a teacher come from God: for no man can do these miracles that thou doest, except God be with him.
3 Jesus answered and said unto him, Verily, verily, I say unto thee, Except a man be born again, he cannot see the kingdom of God.
4 Nicodemus saith unto him, How can a man be born when he is old? can he enter the second time into his mother's womb, and be born?
5 Jesus answered, Verily, verily, I say unto thee, Except a man be

born of water and of the Spirit, he cannot enter into the kingdom of God.

6   That which is born of the flesh is flesh; and that which is born of the Spirit is spirit.

7   Marvel not that I said unto thee, Ye must be born again.

8   The wind bloweth where it listeth, and thou hearest the sound thereof, but canst not tell whence it cometh, and whither it goeth: so is every one that is born of the Spirit.

9   Nicodemus answered and said unto him, How can these things be?

10   Jesus answered and said unto him, Art thou a master of Israel, and knowest not these things?

11   Verily, verily, I say unto thee, We speak that we do know, and testify that we have seen; and ye receive not our witness.

12   If I have told you earthly things, and ye believe not, how shall ye believe, if I tell you of heavenly things?

13   And no man hath ascended up to heaven, but he that came down from heaven, even the Son of man which is in heaven.

14   And as Moses lifted up the serpent in the wilderness, even so must the Son of man be lifted up:

15   That whosoever believeth in him should not perish, but have eternal life.

16   For God so loved the world, that he gave his only begotten Son, that whosoever believeth in him should not perish, but have everlasting life.

17   For God sent not his Son into the world to condemn the world; but that the world through him might be saved.

18   He that believeth on him is not condemned: but he that believeth not is condemned already, because he hath not believed in the name of the only begotten Son of God.

19   And this is the condemnation, that light is come into the world, and men loved darkness rather than light, because their deeds were evil.

20   For every one that doeth evil hateth the light, neither cometh to the light, lest his deeds should be reproved.

21   But he that doeth truth cometh to the light, that his deeds may be made manifest, that they are wrought in God.

Jesus is at His best in His person-to-person encounters, even when some of the disciples are nearby. His patience, understanding, tact and penetration are always evident. But He usually waits for the right opening or lead.

This is demonstrated well in His encounter with Nicodemus, a Pharisee, a leader among the Jews, and belonging to the Sanhedrin. It is a case of the unaccredited teacher instructing one of the best accredited teachers of his day. But Jesus was no bumpkin!

1. We often unwittingly dub the Pharisees as the worst in Judaism. But this is not true; they were among the best.

To be sure, this group hounded Jesus a fair bit, especially for His miracles and "works" on the Sabbath Day. In many areas they were legalists and even Jesus pointed out that they were sometimes hypocritical, especially when they missed the spirit of the law that was involved.

Actually, there were only approximately 6,000 Pharisees in Jesus' day. They were the first to persecute and then prosecute Jesus, and they were some of the first to detect that Jesus was making himself, in some measure, equal with God; and therefore, they thought, He was blaspheming. In the end, it was the Sadducees and Temple priests who really organized the team and mustered their relentless strategy that finally put Jesus on the Cross. Theirs was hatred fed by their entrenched wickedness and corruption, all in the name of religion.

2. Nicodemus sought out Jesus *by night.* Some think that it was in a tent that he found the Galilean teacher, more or less alone. Some think it was in a garden, a favorite place where He would hide out, that these two teachers had their *tête-à-tête.* In saluting Jesus, Nicodemus acknowledged him as "Rabbi" and as "a teacher come from God; for no one can do these signs that you do, unless God is with him." (2, RSV). In turn, Jesus seemed to identify this visitor as a skillful teacher himself by reputation and standing.

Jesus offered His first "salvo" in the encounter, "Truly, truly [meaning Amen, Amen], I say unto you, unless one is born anew [again], he cannot see the kingdom of God" (3, RSV). He was really saying to Nicodemus, "You are not really in; it is a new order of things that is needed, like a new birth." From the outset we discover the poverty of human language and the limitations of given figures or symbols and illustrations.

Paul Scherer, commenting on Jesus' first salute to Nicodemus, observes, "In this . . . a whole new order of life has erupted into history. . . . It was like having all the props knocked out from under you (from where Nicodemus stood), because the things you had counted on were wrong things." (Then almost under his breath Scherer confesses, "We, too, must be stopped in our tracks every day we live by the radical demand which Christ always makes.")[9]

3. But Nicodemus replied in astonishment, and his first word was its key, "How?" It meant, "Impossible!" Then he outlined the process of natural birth and wondered if it could be repeated in an old man like himself.

Jesus proceeded to explain these two orders of life to be considered: one that was in the realm of the flesh, and the other in the realm of the spirit. Morgan summarizes Jesus' words, "Do not confuse flesh with spirit. The spirit of a man may be regenerated; he can be born again."[10]

Nicodemus' next key word is "How" again. But this time he is asking for the working process involved. Jesus chides the accredited teacher with, "What! Is this famous teacher of Israel ignorant of such things?" (10, NEB). Then Jesus identified himself as the Son of Man who came from heaven and implied that He could be relied upon. He said, "We speak what we do know, and bear witness to what we have seen" (11, RSV).

4. But Jesus' real reply to Nicodemus' heart conundrum was the classical story of the fiery serpents in the wilderness who had caused so much death in their ranks and their ensuing cure as directed by God through Moses. Moses made a bronze serpent erected on a pole (or standard), so that anyone who had been bitten could look at it and recover (live) (Num. 21:9, NEB). Thus deliverance followed. Now Jesus points out, "As Moses lifted up the serpent in the wilderness, so must the Son of man be lifted up, that whoever believes in him may have eternal life" (14-15, RSV). This key reference undoubtedly is directed toward Jesus being "lifted up" on the Cross. The goal of eternal life is mentioned for the first time in John's Gospel, but it actually occurs some 16 times in this Book.

5. The ensuing lines constitute one of the gems of this

Gospel. It ranges wide and deep and high. Superlatives are involved, but no exaggerations. John 3:16 has been identified by Robertson as "The Little Gospel" and is often said to be "The Gospel in a Nutshell." We think it is better to join verse 17 with it to get the proper sweep and perspective. Morris is careful to point out that here "the cross is not said to show the love of the Son (as in Gal. 2:20), but that of the Father. The atonement proceeds from the loving heart of God. It is not wrung from Him."[11]

"Believing" is the primary condition of eternal life (a new quality of life that is unending). In redemption God's goal is not judgment (or condemnation), "but that the world might be saved through him."

Here the scope of redemption includes all mankind—"the world." This is true even though the strategy of beginning and organization was in a small land, with a chosen group, many of whom could be readily classed as "provincial." John saw clearly the divine intention and summarizes it well in verse 16. The inspired writer seems to say: *(a)* God cares; *(b)* God communicates; *(c)* God is to be trusted—that is what believing means.

Jesus also faces the alternative to believing, namely, unbelieving. Even in redemption God does not cancel what He did in creation in making man in His own image. Whatever else "his own image" means, it includes the alternative of saying "no" as well as "yes." Love is never coercive. No true fellowship could live in that atmosphere.

6. In the divine strategy of the economy of grace, God's elections are for inclusion and not for exclusion. The apostle John is careful to point out the true key to the unbelieving heart is his own sins. John writes: "Here lies the test: the light has come into the world, but men preferred darkness to light because their deeds were evil. Bad men all hate the light and avoid it, for fear their practices should be shown up. The honest man comes to the light so that it may be clearly seen that God is in all he does" (19-21, NEB).

Clearly, there is an ethical approach to truth, and conversely, there is an unethical approach to evil or sin or spiritual darkness.

We have no written evidence from John that Nicodemus "came into the light" at this time. But later evidence shows him coming through when he joined Joseph of Arimathea in recovering the body of Jesus. Love shone through in that tender ministry in that dark hour. The Galileean conquered even by His death!

John Again Bears Witness to Jesus

John 3:22-36

22 After these things came Jesus and his disciples into the land of Judaea; and there he tarried with them, and baptized.
23 And John also was baptizing in Aenon near to Salim, because there was much water there: and they came, and were baptized.
24 For John was not yet cast into prison.
25 Then there arose a question between some of John's disciples and the Jews about purifying.
26 And they came unto John, and said unto him, Rabbi, he that was with thee beyond Jordan, to whom thou barest witness, behold, the same baptizeth, and all men come to him.
27 John answered and said, A man can receive nothing, except it be given him from heaven.
28 Ye yourselves bear me witness, that I said, I am not the Christ, but that I am sent before him.
29 He that hath the bride is the bridegroom: but the friend of the bridegroom, which standeth and heareth him, rejoiceth greatly because of the bridegroom's voice: this my joy therefore is fulfilled.
30 He must increase, but I must decrease.
31 He that cometh from above is above all: he that is of the earth is earthly, and speaketh of the earth: he that cometh from heaven is above all.
32 And what he hath seen and heard, that he testifieth; and no man receiveth his testimony.
33 He that hath received his testimony hath set to his seal that God is true.
34 For he whom God hath sent speaketh the words of God: for God giveth not the Spirit by measure unto him.
35 The Father loveth the Son, and hath given all things into his hand.
36 He that believeth on the Son hath everlasting life: and he that believeth not the Son shall not see life; but the wrath of God abideth on him.

In our previous word about John the Baptist we were careful to indicate that Jesus' characterization of him was a tribute of high order. In the climax of that sweeping tribute Jesus had identified John as "much more than a prophet." The significance that we read here is that John was the last and climax of the Old Testament prophets. Then when Jesus added, "Yet he who is least in the kingdom of God is greater than he" (Luke 7:28b, RSV), Jesus is referring to a new order that He himself was inaugurating that would transcend and surpass the old. But this was not meant to detract from the effective message and mission of John the Baptist.

1. It was the Baptist's own followers who complained to their master about the success of Jesus' ministry and His increasing following. (This was just before John's imprisonment.) The Baptist rises to the occasion with clarity and dignity in reply, "No one can receive anything except what is given him from heaven. You yourselves bear me witness, that I said I am not the Christ, but I have been sent before him" (27-28, RSV). John's disciples had begun to feel some resentment toward Jesus, ". . . here he is, baptizing, and all are going to him" (26b, RSV).

G. Campbell Morgan calls this and the words that follow "The Recessional of the Herald."[12] John calls for "a recognition of the final, ultimate authority of heaven. . . . It forevermore sweeps out all possibility of rivalry, and all sense that some piece of work is more important than some other."

2. Then the Baptist turns to the custom of those Eastern lands in current use to the office of "the friend of the bridegroom." His chief task was to ceremonially hand the bride over to her groom. John spoke of himself with respect to Christ as "the friend of the Bridegroom." He announced he had heard the Bridegroom's voice and added, "Therefore this joy of mine is now full" (29b, RSV). But the climax of the Baptist's self-effacement comes with majesty, "He must increase, but I must decrease" (30). How many of us could use those words as a daily motto and a sound philosophy for life!

3. Some scholars think that John the Apostle makes his own observations (31-36) and affords an additional perspective to the Baptist's clear reply. The apostle here seems to identify the Baptist as "one that is of the earth, and of the earth he speaks." In contrast, Jesus is "He who comes from heaven and is above all" (31, RSV). Then he applies it to His message and mission, "He who receives his testimony sets his seal to this, that God is true." Morgan points out, "In Jesus such a man finds the Yea and the Amen (the confirmation) to every message of God, and to every covenant of God."[13] It also follows: "For he whom God has sent utters the words of God, for it is not by measure that he gives the Spirit; the Father loves the Son, and has given all things into his hand" (34-35, RSV). Here the resourcefulness of the Son and the authority of the Son measure in comparable strength. Paul's word to the church at Colosse shines here with illumination and corroboration, "For in him the whole fulness of deity dwells bodily, and you have come to fulness of life in him, who is the head of all rule and authority" (Col. 2:9, RSV).

4. John the Apostle closes this section with (what Morgan calls the Processional), "He who believes in the Son has eternal life; he who does not obey the Son shall not see life, but the wrath of God rests upon him" (36, RSV), It is noteworthy that both the RSV and the NEB translate "That believeth not" into "does not obey," suggesting an unethical tone to unbelief.

What an assurance in this Processional that God means what He says and does what He promises! In fact, John Wesley always insisted that God's commands were (actually) only "covered promises." But God is also both honest and fair with us in stating the outcome of spiritual failure born of disobedience. Mayfield quotes in his commentary on John in this section (from Gossip's "Exposition of John," *The Interpreter's Bible*, p. 519): "Christ is never kinder than when his eyes, as he looks at us, are as a flame of fire, and he speaks to us terrible words; when he will make no compromise with us, but demands instant obedience, here and now, on pain of parting with him. If he had not loved us enough to be severe with us, he would have lost our souls. With awe and humility we need to give God thanks no less really for his wrath than for his mercy."

JOHN 4

A Samaritan Woman in Need

John 4:1-42

1 When therefore the Lord knew how the Pharisees had heard that Jesus made and baptized more disciples than John,
2 (Though Jesus himself baptized not, but his disciples,)
3 He left Judaea, and departed again into Galilee.
4 And he must needs go through Samaria.
5 Then cometh he to a city of Samaria, which is called Sychar, near to the parcel of ground that Jacob gave to his son Joseph.
6 Now Jacob's well was there. Jesus therefore, being wearied with his journey, sat thus on the well: and it was about the sixth hour.
7 There cometh a woman of Samaria to draw water: Jesus saith unto her, Give me to drink.
8 (For his disciples were gone away unto the city to buy meat.)
9 Then saith the woman of Samaria unto him, How is it that thou, being a Jew, askest drink of me, which am a woman of Samaria? for the Jews have no dealings with the Samaritans.
10 Jesus answered and said unto her, If thou knewest the gift of God, and who it is that saith to thee, Give me to drink; thou wouldest have asked of him, and he would have given thee living water.
11 The woman saith unto him, Sir, thou hast nothing to draw with, and the well is deep: from whence then hast thou that living water?
12 Art thou greater than our father Jacob, which gave us the well, and drank thereof himself, and his children, and his cattle?
13 Jesus answered and said unto her, Whosoever drinketh of this water shall thirst again:
14 But whosoever drinketh of the water that I shall give him shall never thirst; but the water that I shall give him shall be in him a well of water springing up into everlasting life.
15 The woman saith unto him, Sir, give me this water, that I thirst not, neither come hither to draw.
16 Jesus saith unto her, Go, call thy husband, and come hither.
17 The woman answered and said, I have no husband. Jesus said unto her, Thou hast well said, I have no husband:
18 For thou hast had five husbands; and he whom thou now hast is not thy husband: in that saidst thou truly.
19 The woman saith unto him, Sir I perceive that thou art a prophet.
20 Our fathers worshipped in this mountain; and ye say, that in Jerusalem is the place where men ought to worship.
21 Jesus saith unto her, Woman, believe me, the hour cometh, when

ye shall neither in this mountain, nor yet at Jerusalem, worship the
Father.

22 Ye worship ye know not what: we know what we worship: for salvation is of the Jews.

23 But the hour cometh, and now is, when the true worshippers shall
worship the Father in spirit and in truth: for the Father seeketh such
to worship him.

24 God is a Spirit: and they that worship him must worship him in
spirit and in truth.

25 The woman saith unto him, I know that Messias cometh, which
is called Christ: when he is come, he will tell us all things.

26 Jesus saith unto her, I that speak unto thee am he.

27 And upon this came his disciples, and marvelled that he talked
with the woman: yet no man said, What seekest thou? or, Why talkest
thou with her?

28 The woman then left her waterpot, and went her way into the city,
and saith to the men,

29 Come, see a man, which told me all things that ever I did: is not
this the Christ?

30 Then they went out of the city, and came unto him.

31 In the mean while his disciples prayed him, saying, Master, eat.

32 But he said unto them, I have meat to eat that ye know not of.

33 Therefore said the disciples one to another, Hath any man brought
him ought to eat?

34 Jesus saith unto them, My meat is to do the will of him that sent
me, and to finish his work.

35 Say not ye, There are yet four months, and then cometh harvest?
behold, I say unto you, Lift up your eyes, and look on the fields; for
they are white already to harvest.

36 And he that reapeth receiveth wages, and gathereth fruit unto life
eternal: that both he that soweth and he that reapeth may rejoice together.

37 And herein is that saying true, One soweth, and another reapeth.

38 I sent you to reap that whereon ye bestowed no labour: other men
laboured, and ye are entered into their labors.

39 And many of the Samaritans of that city believed on him for the
saying of the woman, which testified, He told me all that ever I did.

40 So when the Samaritans were come unto him, they besought him
that he would tarry with them: and he abode there two days.

41 And many more believed because of his own word;

42 And said unto the woman, Now we believe, not because of thy saying: for we have heard him ourselves, and know that this is indeed the
Christ, the Saviour of the world.

In Jesus' encounter with the Samaritan woman, we
are not sure what issues were involved in leading the Master to take the shortcut through Samaria rather than the
usual route around it. Actually, Jesus lost time in His
journey to Galilee via the shorter route, for His two-day
stopover delayed Him finally. After the Samaritan woman
had reported to her own people about Jesus, they pressed
Him to stay. G. Campbell Morgan points out that "our

Lord is seen crossing the boundary line of prejudice, and supposed privilege as he went through Samaria."[14]

We should recall, however, that when Jesus sent out the original Twelve, He outlined the strategy of their mission: "Go nowhere among the Gentiles, and enter no town of the Samaritans, but go rather to the lost sheep of the house of Israel" (Matt. 10:5-6, RSV). Later on, these limitations were removed and their field of service expanded to include "Samaria, and away to the ends of the earth" (Acts 1:8, NEB).

The sharp strain existing between Jews and Samaritans is well highlighted by a clash Jesus had with the leaders of Jewry later on. He had prodded them and asked why they planned to kill Him, principally for giving them the truth. Their bitter reply was, "Are we not right in saying that you are a Samaritan and have a demon?" (John 8:48, RSV).

1. Jesus' meeting with the Samaritan woman came about in a natural way. He was tired and sat by Jacob's well to rest while His disciples went to buy provisions. This Samaritan woman came along at the noon hour with her bucket to draw water. Jesus requested a drink, for He was also thirsty. The woman herself was taken aback at Jesus' request, for she was aware of the constant strain between Jews and Samaritans. No doubt she was familiar with the Jews' hesitance about using vessels that Samaritans had previously used. When she demurred, Jesus volunteered, "If only you knew what God gives, and who it is that is asking for a drink, you would have asked him, and he would have given living water" (10, NEB). Without hesitation the woman replied, "Sir, you have no bucket and the well is deep. How can you give me 'living water'? Are you greater than Jacob, our ancestor, who gave us the well and drank from it himself . . . ?" (12-17, NEB).

Jesus seized the initiative next and pointed out the difference between the water from Jacob's well and the "living water" He had in mind. He insisted that in the use of Jacob's well water, one's thirst would recur after drinking, but "whoever drinks the water that I shall give him will never suffer thirst any more. The water that I shall give him will be an inner spring always welling up for eternal life" (14, NEB). Without further comprehension, the woman blurted out, "Sir . . . give me that water, and then I shall not be thirsty, nor have to come all this way to draw" (15, NEB).

2. At this point, Jesus "dropped the bomb"! In an almost staccato outline, He replied, "Go home, call your husband and come back" (16, NEB). What an outline! It related to her deepest need. He read clearly her wretchedness, but He knew she must relate it to God's moral order. By her acknowledgment of sin God could grant her forgiveness and peace.

   Still she held out. Her reply was evasive, almost petulant: "I have no husband." Jesus pursued her need, like "the Hound of Heaven," with: "You are right in saying that you have no husband, for, although you have had five husbands, the man with whom you are now living is not your husband; you told the truth there" (17-18, NEB). By now the woman must have felt badly "shattered" inwardly. Jowett observes here, "For sin had been blazing in the secret place, and had scorched the delicacies of the spirit. . . . Her heart was like some charred chamber after a destructive fire."[15]

3. The woman ventured with, "Sir, I can see that you are a prophet" (19, RSV). Then she suddenly resorted to a ploy and asked who was right with regard to the place of worship, the Samaritans or the Jews. Jesus did not tarry here long—it was not her real issue. He did point out, "You Samaritans worship without knowing what you worship, while we worship what we know. It is from the Jews that salvation comes" (22, NEB). Actually, Jesus knew that the Samaritans were idolators but He did go to the heart of the meaning of worship in His word to this strug-

gling woman. Here He gives one of His two greatest tributes concerning the person and work of God that John records. He declares with the elegance and simplicity of one who knew: "The time . . . is already here when those who are real worshippers will worship the Father in spirit and in truth. Such are the worshippers whom the Father wants" (23, NEB). Jesus was saying, There is no inner reality in religion without sincerity and *absolute honesty* with God.

Presently the woman expressed her faith in the coming Messiah and that He would eventually tell them everything. Without a prelude Jesus said to her, "I am he, I who am speaking to you now" (6, NEB). What a revelation to a struggling woman! Only the Son of God could have had humility enough to make such a revelation, to such a woman at such a time!

4. At this juncture, the disciples returned and were dumbfounded that Jesus had been speaking to a Samaritan woman alone. But they maintained a discreet silence. Presently they urged Him to eat something, but He replied, "I have food that you know nothing about. . . . It is meat and drink for me to do the will of him who sent me until I have finished his work" (32, 34, NEB).

5. Meanwhile the woman put down her water jug in a hurry and went to her own people and said, "Come see a man who has told me everything I ever did. Could this be the Messiah?" (29, NEB). The Samaritans then came and pressed Jesus to stay and He spent two days longer there. They believed and confessed, for they had heard Jesus for themselves. They added, "And we know that this is in truth the Saviour of the world" (42b, NEB). What a witness and what a title from recent converts! In commenting on the change wrought among the Samaritans, Roy L. Smith observes, "The one sufficient authentication of our Christian faith is the changed lives it produces. If the church can go on pouring saints into this world's life its

future is assured. If it ever ceases to do this, then no theology will save it."[16]

Our soul sings to God today—alone in our study—that wonderful hymn, written some two centuries ago:

Come, Thou Fount of ev'ry blessing,
Tune my heart to sing Thy grace.
Streams of mercy, never ceasing,
Call for songs of loudest praise.
Teach me some melodious sonnet,
Sung by flaming tongues above.
Praise the mount! I'm fixed upon it,
Mount of God's unchanging love.

Oh, to grace how great a debtor
Daily I'm constrained to be!
Let that grace now, like a fetter,
Bind my yielded heart to Thee.
Let my know Thee in Thy fullness;
Guide me by Thy mighty hand
Till, transformed, in Thine own image
In Thy presence I shall stand.

—ROBERT ROBINSON

Healing of the Nobleman's Son: The Second Sign

John 4:43-54

43 Now after two days he departed thence, and went into Galilee.
44 For Jesus himself testified, that a prophet hath no honour in his own country.
45 Then when he was come into Galilee, the Galilaeans received him, having seen all the things that he did at Jerusalem at the feast: for they also went unto the feast.
46 So Jesus came again into Cana of Galilee, where he made the water wine. And there was a certain nobleman, whose son was sick at Capernaum.
47 When he heard that Jesus was come out of Judaea into Galilee, he went unto him, and besought him that he would come down, and heal his son: for he was at the point of death.
48 Then said Jesus unto him, Except ye see signs and wonders, ye will not believe.
49 The nobleman saith unto him, Sir, come down ere my child die.
50 Jesus saith unto him, Go thy way; thy son liveth. And the man believed the word that Jesus had spoken unto him, and he went his way.

51 And as he was now going down, his servants met him, and told him, saying, Thy son liveth.
52 Then enquired he of them the hour when he began to amend. And they said unto him, Yesterday at the seventh hour the fever left him.
53 So the father knew that it was at the same hour, in the which Jesus said unto him, Thy son liveth: and himself believed, and his whole house.
54 This is again the second miracle that Jesus did, when he was come out of Judaea into Galilee.

The story of the healing of the nobleman's son is almost a casual thing the way it came about. John does not call these healings miracles as do the Synoptists. He calls them "signs" or "works." This particular one is identified as the second sign, and the word of assurance was spoken by Jesus in Cana of Galilee, where the first sign was given at a wedding feast.

1. The man involved was a servant of Herod the Tetrarch, a title comparable to a governor. The man traveled some 15 miles from Capernaum to find Jesus. His plea was urgent, for his son was dying with an acute fever. Nothing else was important to that man just then.

At first, Jesus seemed to be reluctant to help, for He knew the man's request meant, "Go with me to Capernaum and heal him." Jesus tested the father with, "Will none of you ever believe without seeing signs and portents?" (49, NEB). The man hung on. Barclay translates his term for his boy as "my little lad."

Presently Jesus said, "Return home, your son will live" (50a, NEB). The record follows: "The man believed what Jesus had said and started for home" (50b, NEB).

2. Those must have seemed long miles that afternoon, but before the father got home his servants met him outside the city with the good news that his son was alive. (The Irish would have added, "and doing bravely!") The nobleman checked the hour when the fever left the lad and the word was at one in the afternoon. Sure enough, that was exactly the hour when Jesus had sent him home with assurance! The story closes with, ". . . and he [the father] and all his household became believers" (53b, NEB).

Healing the Derelict: The Third Sign

John 5:1-18

1 After this there was a feast of the Jews; and Jesus went up to Jerusalem.

2 Now there is at Jerusalem by the sheep market a pool, which is called in the Hebrew tongue Bethesda, having five porches.

3 In these lay a great multitude of impotent folk, of blind, halt, withered, waiting for the moving of the water.

4 For an angel went down at a certain season into the pool, and troubled the water: whosoever then first after the troubling of the water stepped in was made whole of whatsoever disease he had.

5 And a certain man was there, which had an infirmity thirty and eight years.

6 When Jesus saw him lie, and knew that he had been now a long time in that case, he saith unto him, Wilt thou be made whole?

7 The impotent man answered him, Sir, I have no man, when the water is troubled, to put me into the pool: but while I am coming, another steppeth down before me.

8 Jesus saith unto him, Rise, take up thy bed, and walk.

9 And immediately the man was made whole, and took up his bed, and walked: and on the same day was the sabbath.

10 The Jews therefore said unto him that was cured, It is the sabbath day: it is not lawful for thee to carry thy bed.

11 He answered them, He that made me whole, the same said unto me, Take up thy bed, and walk.

12 Then asked they him, What man is that which said unto thee, Take up thy bed, and walk?

13 And he that was healed wist not who it was: for Jesus had conveyed himself away, a multitude being in that place.

14 Afterward Jesus findeth him in the temple, and said unto him, Behold, thou art made whole: sin no more, lest a worse thing come unto thee.

15 The man departed, and told the Jews that it was Jesus, which had made him whole.

16 And therefore did the Jews persecute Jesus, and sought to slay him, because he had done these things on the sabbath day.

17 But Jesus answered them, My Father worketh hitherto, and I work.

18 Therefore the Jews sought the more to kill him, because he not only had broken the sabbath, but said also that God was his Father, making himself equal with God.

The healing of the cripple, whom we have chosen to call a derelict, is a classic example of the conflict with the Jews that was developing in the Master's ministry. It was Jesus' compassion and perception versus the multiplied rules and legalism of the Jews. Even in the prologue John had outlined it, "He came to his own home, and his own people received him not" (1:11, RSV).

Jesus actually was beginning His second year of His ministry about now. The feast involved could have been the Passover. His first year had been relatively obscure, but this healing came as a portent of the conflict that would soon break upon Him with increasing and deepening strength. Morgan observes in quick summary. "On the human level, what Jesus did that day, and what He said that day, cost Him His life. They never forgave Him."[17]

1. It was Jesus who took the initiative in this cure. (God *always* does that!) This cripple was at least partially paralyzed, had been helpless for some 38 years. He was actually a beggar by trade. Jesus saw him in the crowd of sick people—blind, lame, and paralyzed. He challenged him with, "Do you want to be healed?" (6, RSV) The man complained in reply that he had no one to help him into the pool when the waters "were troubled." There was supposed to be healing in the water's minerals and "bubbles." But the man whined that always someone else got in ahead of him because he was so slow. Jesus then made that seemingly impossible demand of the cripple: "Rise, take up your pallet, and walk." The record follows: "And at once the man was healed, and he took up his pallet and walked" (9, RSV). Then Jesus slipped out of sight.

2. The Jews saw this renewed man carrying his pallet on the Sabbath Day and reminded him that this was against the law. (The truth was such violations were punishable by death by stoning.) The Jews probably warned him of this. The man replied, "The man who healed me said to me, 'Take up your pallet and walk'" (11, RSV). But the man couldn't identify his benefactor. Later, Jesus found the man in the Temple, and said to him, "See, you are well! Sin no more, that nothing worse befall you" (14, NEB). This was the real reason for his healing. Jesus wanted his direction changed from within so that he would be

at home with God, instead of continuing as a wanderer and a vagabond.

Then the ungrateful derelict went and identified Jesus by name to the Jews. (The man could see himself with rocks piled upon him outside of the city, if the Jewish leaders carried out their threat against him!)

Meanwhile the Jews began the follow-up on Jesus, for they sought to kill Him.

Jesus knew the man had to "break" with sin, that it could not be whittled off in slivers. It had to be a radical break. That is why Jesus sought him out in the Temple.

A Discourse of Jesus: A Response

John 5:19-47

19 Then answered Jesus and said unto them, Verily, verily, I say unto you, The Son can do nothing of himself, but what he seeth the Father do: for what things soever he doeth, these also doeth the Son likewise.

20 For the Father loveth the Son, and sheweth him all things that himself doeth: and he will shew him greater works than these, that ye may marvel.

21 For as the Father raiseth up the dead, and quickeneth them; even so the Son quickeneth whom he will.

22 For the Father judgeth no man, but hath committed all judgment unto the Son:

23 That all men should honour the Son, even as they honour the Father. He that honoureth not the Son honoureth not the Father which hath sent him.

24 Verily, verily, I say unto you, He that heareth my word, and believeth on him that sent me, hath everlasting life, and shall not come into condemnation; but is passed from death unto life.

25 Verily, verily, I say unto you, The hour is coming, and now is, when the dead shall hear the voice of the Son of God: and they that hear shall live.

26 For as the Father hath life in himself; so hath he given to the Son to have life in himself;

27 And hath given him authority to execute judgment also, because he is the Son of man.

28 Marvel not at this: for the hour is coming, in the which all that are in the graves shall hear his voice,

29 And shall come forth; they that have done good, unto the resurrection of life; and they that have done evil, unto the resurrection of damnation.

30 I can of mine own self do nothing: as I hear, I judge: and my judgment is just; because I seek not mine own will, but the will of the Father which hath sent me.

31 If I bear witness of myself, my witness is not true.

32 There is another that beareth witness of me; and I know that the witness which he witnesseth of me is true.

33 Ye sent unto John, and he bare witness unto the truth.
34 But I receive not testimony from man: but these things I say, that ye might be saved.
35 He was a burning and a shining light: and ye were willing for a season to rejoice in his light.
36 But I have greater witness than that of John: for the works which the Father hath given me to finish, the same works that I do, bear witness of me, that the Father hath sent me.
37 And the Father himself, which hath sent me, hath borne witness of me. Ye have neither heard his voice at any time, nor seen his shape.
38 And ye have not his word abiding in you: for whom he hath sent, him ye believe not.
39 Search the scriptures; for in them ye think ye have eternal life: and they are they which testify of me.
40 And ye will not come to me, that ye might have life.
41 I receive not honour from men.
42 But I know you, that ye have not the love of God in you.
43 I am come in my Father's name, and ye receive me not: if another shall come in his own name, him ye will receive.
44 How can ye believe, which receive honour one of another, and seek not the honour that cometh from God only?
45 Do not think that I will accuse you to the Father: there is one that accuseth you, even Moses in whom ye trust.
46 For had ye believed Moses, ye would have believed me: for he wrote of me.
47 But if ye believe not his writings, how shall ye believe my words?

In the preceding miracle Jesus had actually stirred up deep animosity among these leading Jews, until they were ready to stone Him to death. This is probably the first time that the apostle John records such strong opposition to Jesus.

It was a strange scene, to witness the healing of a lifetime cripple at the word of Jesus; then to observe the bitterness that enshrouds Jesus by His own people, the Jews. His redemptive mission was spoiled for them because it was done on the Sabbath. Augustine comments on this: "They sought darkness from the Sabbath more than light from the miracle."

In addition to the healing, Jesus had been true to the derelict after his healing and had admonished him to turn away from sin ("Sin no more") lest a worse plight should come upon him. Now the compassion and love of redemption is swallowed up in the alchemy of hate.

1. John explains the new confrontation swiftly, namely, "because he [Jesus] not only broke the sabbath but also

called God his own Father, making himself equal to God" (18, RSV). This unique Sonship that Jesus claimed was blasphemy and worthy of death, according to these Jews.

Jesus' reply was more than casual; everything was at stake. He insisted that His conduct was patterned after the Father's. He imitated Him, for Their unity was unbroken.

Three times in His conversation Jesus employed the double "Truly, truly," which really meant "Amen, amen." This expression was an emphatic reassurance of truth, based on the reliability of God himself.

2. Jesus also reported several witnesses who could corroborate His claims. These included: *(a)* John the Baptist, whom they had followed for a while (32-33); *(b)* the very works which He had done testified to the Father's enablement which He enjoyed (36); *(c)* the witness of the Father himself (37); *(d)* the Scriptures that they had studied so studiously also bore witness concerning Him (39); and *(e)* Moses likewise wrote concerning Him (46).

3. Then Jesus probed for the inner reason that provoked their clash with Him. He pointed out carefully: *(a)* the Father's voice you have never heard (37); *(b)* the Father's word does not abide in you, for you do not believe Him (Jesus) whom He has sent (38); *(c)* you do not have the love of God within you (42); *(d)* your unbelief comes from mutual self-seeking and your self-glorifying.

4. Out of all this clash and bitterness, could we not find gems of truth for our own lives in our day? Here is one. Jesus said: "My judgment is just [true, sound], because I seek not mine own will, but the will of him who sent me" (30, RSV). Is there not a practical sense in which we could apply this principle to our own life-style? Would it not offer us guidance, perspective, direction, and peace? Amen. The step from criticism to worship is shorter than we think if we'll be honest with ourselves and dare to face up to God's demands.

JOHN 6

Feeding of the Five Thousand: The Fourth Sign

John 6:1-14

1 After these things Jesus went over the sea of Galilee, which is the sea of Tiberias.

2 And a great multitude followed him, because they saw his miracles which he did on them that were diseased.

3 And Jesus went up into a mountain, and there he sat with his disciples.

4 And the passover, a feast of the Jews, was nigh.

5 When Jesus then lifted up his eyes, and saw a great company come unto him, he saith unto Philip, Whence shall we buy bread, that these may eat?

6 And this he said to prove him: for he himself knew what he would do.

7 Philip answered him, Two hundred pennyworth of bread is not sufficient for them, that every one of them may take a little.

8 One of his disciples, Andrew, Simon Peter's brother, saith unto him,

9 There is a lad here, which hath five barley loaves, and two small fishes: but what are they among so many?

10 And Jesus said, Make the men sit down. Now there was much grass in the place. So the men sat down, in number about five thousand.

11 And Jesus took the loaves; and when he had given thanks, he distributed to the disciples, and the disciples to them that were set down; and likewise of the fishes as much as they would.

12 When they were filled, he said unto his disciples, Gather up the fragments that remain, that nothing be lost.

13 Therefore they gathered them together, and filled twelve baskets with the fragments of the five barley loaves, which remained over and above unto them that had eaten.

14 Then those men, when they had seen the miracle that Jesus did, said, This is of a truth that prophet that should come into the world.

The feeding of the 5,000 is the only miracle, apart from the Resurrection, that is recorded in all four Gospels. It cannot be explained apart from the love and power of God, manifested through His Son. It was also another "sign" in the unfolding and ongoing of Jesus' messianic mission. Even at the close of that luncheon, some would have given Him a place as "Exalted Restaurateur," but Jesus quickly identified them as freeloaders.

Just prior to the feast, John the Baptist had been slain at the behest of a bad woman (and man) whose sin the Baptist had denounced. We are convinced that the loss of John, the Voice, had "shaken" Jesus considerably, so that He sought the isolation of quiet and prayer. Nevertheless, the crowd followed Him, for His camp followers were increasing constantly.

1. It was as He looked on this large crowd that Jesus was moved with compassion, for many had walked long distances to hear Him and to see Him. He turned to Philip (who could have been the steward of provisions in their group) and inquired, "Where are we to buy bread to feed these people?" (5, NEB). John notes, "This he said to test him, for he himself knew what he would do" (6, RSV). Philip's reply was, "Two hundred denarii would not buy enough bread for each of them to have a little." The researchers advise us that a denarius then amounted to a day's wages for a laborer.

(See appendix for a sermon outline on John 6:6)

2. Presently, Andrew moved in on the scene. He suggested with some trepidation, "There is a lad here who has five barley loaves (the cheapest bread) and two fish; but what are they among so many?" (9, RSV). It was a case of "a 'wee' boy's lunch to feed a big crowd!" However, sometimes small boys eat big lunches!

One minister was preaching on this miracle and insisted that at first glance he thought there were two miracles here. The first one was the fact that the lad had not already eaten his own lunch!

3. Then Jesus instructed the disciples to organize the people on the grass, and so the great mass was sorted out into orderly companies, and the number of men was 5,000.

Jesus gave thanks before the distribution started. It was done, bread first and then the fish, in order. There was no "quota"; "as much as they wanted" was the rule (11, RSV). They didn't finish until all "had eaten their fill." Jesus followed this by a conservation move, "Gather up the fragments left over that nothing be lost" (12, RSV). Those who gathered the fragments reported 12 baskets full. Some scholar has suggested that each of the apostles had a basket full to himself. If so, we hope Andrew remembered that "wee" boy who gave up his own whole lunch to the proposition.

4. The outcome of this miracle was that the general word went around, "This is of a truth that Prophet that should come into the world" (14). Then Jesus became aware of a growing clamor among the crowd to seize Him and make Him king, regardless. So He "withdrew again to the hills by himself" (15, NEB). R. F. Bailey points up the irony of this situation, "He who is already King has come to open up His kingdom to men; but in their blindness men try to force Him to be the kind of king they want; thus they fail to get the king they want, and also lose the kingdom He offers."[1]

Jesus Walks on the Water: The Fifth Sign

John 6:15-21

> 15 When Jesus therefore perceived that they would come and take him by force, to make him a king, he departed again into a mountain himself alone.
> 16 And when even was now come, his disciples went down unto the sea,
> 17 And entered into a ship, and went over the sea toward Capernaum. And it was now dark, and Jesus was not come to them.
> 18 And the sea arose by reason of a great wind that blew.
> 19 So when they had rowed about five and twenty or thirty furlongs, they see Jesus walking on the sea, and drawing nigh unto the ship: and they were afraid.
> 20 But he saith unto them, It is I; be not afraid.
> 21 Then they willingly received him into the ship: and immediately the ship was at the land whither they went.

John's account of Jesus walking on the water is rather summary. No mention is made of Peter's effort to walk on the water. It could be that, here again, John was aware that the Early Church had two previous accounts given of this boat trip. The apostle John seems to be bridging two other events with this outline story.

Jesus had sent His disciples on ahead of Him while He tarried to quiet and disperse the crowd of "kingmakers." Then He slipped off alone to pray. Evidently He had some tentative arrangement to meet His inner group in some region or even at a given time.

The disciples rented or borrowed a boat and a storm hit them furiously. They had rowed strenuously for more than half the night and it was slow going. A fairly large percentage of these disciples could not be classed as land-lubbers. They knew the lake and the area for storms. Presently they saw a Man overtaking them as He walked on the water. The disciples thought it was an apparition or a phantom. They were frightened. Presently, the Man called out, "It is I; be not afraid." It was Jesus.

In Matthew's account, he inserts the part played by Peter. They seemed uneasy about the so-called phantom even though He talked like Jesus. Peter spoke up, "Lord, if it be thou, bid me come unto thee on the water. And he said, Come" (14:28-29). Then Peter got his eyes on the wind and the waves and began to sink until Jesus had to rescue him.

It is Mark's account that closes with, "And they that were in the boat worshipped him, saying, 'Of a truth thou art the Son of God'" (14:33).

John's account closes with tranquility, "Then they were ready to take him [Jesus] aboard, and immediately the boat reached the land they were making for" (6:21, NEB).

Discourse on Jesus the Bread of Life

John 6:22-59

> 22 The day following, when the people which stood on the other side of the sea saw that there was none other boat there, save that one whereinto his disciples were entered, and that Jesus went not with his disciples into the boat, but that his disciples were gone away alone;

23 (Howbeit there came other boats from Tiberias nigh unto the place where they did eat bread, after that the Lord had given thanks:)

24 When the people therefore saw that Jesus was not there, neither his disciples, they also took shipping, and came to Capernaum, seeking for Jesus.

25 And when they had found him on the other side of the sea they said unto him, Rabbi, when camest thou hither?

26 Jesus answered them and said, Verily, verily, I say unto you, Ye seek me, not because ye saw the miracles, but because ye did eat of the loaves, and were filled.

27 Labour not for the meat which perisheth, but for that meat which endureth unto everlasting life, which the Son of man shall give unto you: for him hath God the Father sealed.

28 Then said they unto him, What shall we do, that we might work the work of God?

29 Jesus answered and said unto them, This is the work of God, that ye believe on him whom he hath sent.

30 They said therefore unto him, What sign shewest thou then, that we may see, and believe thee? what dost thou work?

31 Our fathers did eat manna in the desert; as it is written, He gave them bread from heaven to eat.

32 Then Jesus said unto them, Verily, verily, I say unto you, Moses gave you not that bread from heaven; but my Father giveth you the true bread from heaven.

33 For the bread of God is he which cometh down from heaven, and giveth life unto the world.

34 Then said they unto him, Lord, evermore give us this bread.

35 And Jesus said unto them, I am the bread of life: he that cometh to me shall never hunger; and he that believeth on me shall never thirst.

36 But I said unto you, That ye also have seen me, and believe not.

37 All that the Father giveth me shall come to me; and him that cometh to me I will in no wise cast out.

38 For I came down from heaven, not to do mine own will, but the will of him that sent me.

39 And this is the Father's will which hath sent me, that of all which he hath given me I should lose nothing, but should raise it up again at the last day.

40 And this is the will of him that sent me, that every one which seeth the Son, and believeth on him, may have everlasting life: and I will raise him up at the last day.

41 The Jews then murmured at him, because he said, I am the bread which came down from heaven.

42 And they said, Is not this Jesus, the son of Joseph, whose father and mother we know? how is it then that he saith, I came down from heaven?

43 Jesus therefore answered and said unto them, Murmur not among yourselves.

44 No man can come to me, except the Father which hath sent me draw him: and I will raise him up at the last day.

45 It is written in the prophets, And they shall be all taught of God. Every man therefore that hath heard, and hath learned of the Father, cometh unto me.

46 Not that any man hath seen the Father, save he which is of God, he hath seen the Father.

47 Verily, verily, I say unto you, He that believeth on me hath everlasting life.
48 I am that bread of life.
49 Your fathers did eat manna in the wilderness, and are dead.
50 This is the bread which cometh down from heaven, that a man may eat thereof, and not die.
51 I am the living bread which came down from heaven: if any man eat of this bread, he shall live for ever: and the bread that I will give is my flesh, which I will give for the life of the world.
52 The Jews therefore strove among themselves, saying, How can this man give us his flesh to eat?
53 Then Jesus said unto them, Verily, Verily, I say unto you, Except ye eat the flesh of the Son of man, and drink his blood, ye have no life in you.
54 Whoso eateth my flesh, and drinketh my blood, hath eternal life; and I will raise him up at the last day.
55 For my flesh is meat indeed, and my blood is drink indeed.
56 He that eateth my flesh, and drinketh my blood, dwelleth in me, and I in him.
57 As the living Father hath sent me, and I live by the Father: so he that eateth me, even he shall live by me.
58 This is that bread which came down from heaven: not as your fathers did eat manna, and are dead: he that eateth of this bread shall live for ever.
59 These things said he in the synagogue, as he taught in Capernaum.

In the discourse on Jesus as the Bread of Life, the discussion seems to be a bit scattered, but it climaxes in the synagogue in Capernaum. Some of the multitude that had acclaimed Jesus after the feeding of the 5,000 were still seeking Him. When they met they inquired when He got there, but instead He pointed out why they came there. He said, "You seek me, not because you saw signs, but because you ate your fill of loaves" (26b, RSV). He admonished them, "Do not labor for the food which perishes, but for the food which endures to eternal life" (27, RSV). Then they inquired what they must do to carry out the work of God. He answered, "This is the work of God, that you believe in him whom he has sent" (29, RSV). Immediately they wanted a sign that they could see and then believe. They said "What work do you perform?" (30, RSV).

In commenting on this general background, Temple points out, "The miracle of feeding was to them a convenience rather than a revelation."[2] The previous miracle observers now demand a new and greater sign. MacGregor observes carefully, "Christ would produce no credential so conclusive but the Jews would demand one more conclusive still."[3]

1. Jesus listened patiently as they reminded Him how their fathers ate manna in the wilderness. They quoted the scripture, "He gave them bread from heaven to eat" (31). Immediately Jesus pointed out that it was not Moses, but the Father who gave them bread from heaven. Then He added, "My Father gives you the true bread from heaven. For the bread of God is that which comes down from heaven and gives life to the world" (32-33, RSV). Immediately they replied, "Sir, give us this bread now and always" (34, NEB). Jesus continued, "I am the bread of life. Whoever comes to me shall never be hungry, and whoever believes in me shall never be thirsty. But you, as I said, do not believe although you have seen" (35-36, NEB).

2. The Jews "choked" over the fact of Jesus' Person as the Incarnate Son of God. They could only identify Him as the son of Joseph and the child of Mary. But they had a harder time with His coming Passion—His death on the Cross for the sins of the world. This is what He is talking about in those mysterious words that were so shocking to the Jews and raised a fierce dispute among them. Jesus said in explanation: "In truth, in very truth [The Amen and amen] I tell you, unless you eat the flesh of the Son of Man and drink his blood you can have no life in you. Whoever eats my flesh and drinks my blood possesses eternal life, and I will raise him up on the last day. . . . As the living Father sent me, and I live because of the Father, so he who eats me shall live because of me" (53-54, 57, NEB).

We acknowledged in our introduction that John makes no mention of the institution of the Lord's Supper as such, but the above lesson is John's counterpart for Matthew 26:26-29. John's account reads like a sacrament, for it speaks of spiritual reality. It shows us the mystery of His passion well in advance of the Cross. It is not magic nor careless, coarse cannibalism. It is beautiful symbolism that does not carry spiritual benefit apart from simple faith in Jesus Christ the Son, who became our Savior. He alone affords the sacrament. No one can destroy it.

Some Disciples Hesitate; Others Go Back

John 6:60-71

60 Many therefore of his disciples, when they had heard this, said, This is an hard saying; who can hear it?
61 When Jesus knew in himself that his disciples murmured at it, he said unto them, Doth this offend you?
62 What and if ye shall see the Son of man ascend up where he was before?
63 It is the spirit that quickeneth; the flesh profiteth nothing: the words that I speak unto you, they are spirit, and they are life.
64 But there are some of you that believe not. For Jesus knew from the beginning who they were that believed not, and who should betray him.
65 And he said, Therefore said I unto you, that no man can come unto me, except it were given unto him of my Father.
66 From that time many of his disciples went back, and walked no more with him.
67 Then said Jesus unto the twelve, Will ye also go away?
68 Then Simon Peter answered him, Lord, to whom shall we go? thou hast the words of eternal life.
69 And we believe and are sure that thou art that Christ, the Son of the living God.
70 Jesus answered them, Have not I chosen you twelve, and one of you is a devil?
71 He spake of Judas Iscariot the son of Simon: for he it was that should betray him, being one of the twelve.

In this postscript Jesus had discovered some complaining among His disciples over the depth of His Bread of Life discussions. He asked, "Do you take offense at this? Then what if you were to see the Son of Man ascending where he was before?" (61-62, RSV). Quickly He added, "It is the spirit that gives life, the flesh is of no avail; the words that I have spoken unto you are spirit and life" (63, RSV). He then adds a key to the situation when he flatly states that there were some of them "that did not believe, and who it was that should betray him." Here Judas seemed to be the center of unbelief.

The record follows: "After this many of his disciples

drew back and no longer went about with him" (66, RSV). Things were settling down and the wide popularity had begun to dwindle when they realized the rugged path that Jesus had chosen and identified as the will of the Father for Him. At this point Jesus turned to the Twelve and said: "Will you also go away?" "Simon Peter answered him, 'Lord, to whom shall we go? You have the words of eternal life; and we have believed and have come to know, that you are the Holy One of God'" (67-69, RSV).

At this point the Master spoke out with probable solemnity, "Did I not choose you, the twelve, and one of you is a devil?" (70, RSV). John identifies the one of whom Jesus now spoke (without naming him) as Judas, the son of Simon Iscariot. Unbelief had produced a traitor, but Jesus followed him with fidelity and compassion to the end.

JOHN 7

Jesus Hides Out in Galilee

John 7:1-9

> 1 After these things Jesus walked in Galilee: for he would not walk in Jewry, because the Jews sought to kill him.
> 2 Now the Jews' feast of tabernacles was at hand.
> 3 His brethren therefore said unto him, Depart hence, and go into Judaea, that thy disciples also may see the works that thou doest.
> 4 For there is no man that doeth any thing in secret, and he himself seeketh to be known openly. If thou do these things, shew thyself to the world.
> 5 For neither did his brethren believe in him.
> 6 Then Jesus said unto them, My time is not yet come: but your time is alway ready.
> 7 The world cannot hate you; but me it hateth, because I testify of it, that the works thereof are evil.
> 8 Go ye up unto this feast: I go not up yet unto this feast; for my time is not yet full come.
> 9 When he had said these words unto them, he abode still in Galilee.

Jesus' hiding out in Galilee was not born of cowardice; it was His sense of timing that controlled. His time was not yet come (6). His own family (his brothers—probably younger brothers, children of Joseph and Mary) chided Him a bit. It was close to the Jewish Feast of the Tabernacles and they thought He ought to go to Jerusalem and get the exposure. They said, "Surely no one can hope to be in the public eye if he works in seclusion. If you really are doing such things as these, show yourself to the world" (4, NEB). Jesus acknowledged that the world hated Him for exposing the wickedness of its ways.

But He said No now about going to the feast, for He planned to go in secret later on. The current question then at the beginning of the feast was, "Where is He?"

The Feast of Tabernacles: Controversy

John 7:10-36, 45-53

> 10 But when his brethren were gone up, then went he also up unto the feast, not openly, but as it were in secret.
> 11 Then the Jews sought him at the feast, and said, Where is he?
> 12 And there was much murmuring among the people concerning him: for some said, He is a good man: others said, Nay; but he deceiveth the people.
> 13 Howbeit no man spake openly of him for fear of the Jews.
> 14 Now about the midst of the feast Jesus went up into the temple, and taught.
> 15 And the Jews marvelled, saying, How knoweth this man letters, having never learned?
> 16 Jesus answered them, and said, My doctrine is not mine, but his that sent me.
> 17 If any man will do his will, he shall know of the doctrine, whether it be of God, or whether I speak of myself.
> 18 He that speaketh of himself seeketh his own glory: but he that seeketh his glory that sent him, the same is true, and no unrighteousness is in him.
> 19 Did not Moses give you the law, and yet none of you keepeth the law? Why go ye about to kill me?
> 20 The people answered and said, Thou hast a devil: who goeth about to kill thee?
> 21 Jesus answered and said unto them, I have done one work, and ye all marvel.
> 22 Moses therefore gave unto you circumcision; (not because it is of Moses, but of the fathers;) and ye on the sabbath day circumcise a man.
> 23 If a man on the sabbath day receive circumcision, that the law of Moses should not be broken; are ye angry at me, because I have made a man every whit whole on the sabbath day?
> 24 Judge not according to the appearance, but judge righteous judgment.

25 Then said some of them of Jerusalem, Is not this he, whom they seek to kill?
26 But, lo, he speaketh boldly, and they say nothing unto him. Do the rulers know indeed that this is the very Christ?
27 Howbeit we know this man whence he is: but when Christ cometh, no man knoweth whence he is.
28 Then cried Jesus in the temple as he taught, saying, Ye both know me, and ye know whence I am: and I am not come of myself, but he that sent me is true, whom ye know not.
29 But I know him: for I am from him, and he hath sent me.
30 Then they sought to take him: but no man laid hands on him, because his hour was not yet come.
31 And many of the people believed on him, and said, When Christ cometh, will he do more miracles than these which this man hath done?
32 The Pharisees heard that the people murmured such things concerning him; and the Pharisees and the chief priests sent officers to take him.
33 Then said Jesus unto them, Yet a little while am I with you, and then I go unto him that sent me.
34 Ye shall seek me, and shall not find me: and where I am, thither ye cannot come.
35 Then said the Jews among themselves, Whither will he go, that we shall not find him? will he go unto the dispersed among the Gentiles, and teach the Gentiles?
36 What manner of saying is this that he said, Ye shall seek me, and shall not find me: and where I am, thither ye cannot come?

45 Then came the officers to the chief priests and Pharisees; and they said unto them, Why have ye not brought him?
46 The officers answered, Never man spake like this man.
47 Then answered them the Pharisees, Are ye also deceived?
48 Have any of the rulers or of the Pharisees believed on him?
49 But this people who knoweth not the law are cursed.
50 Nicodemus saith unto them, (he that came to Jesus by night, being one of them,)
51 Doth our law judge any man, before it hear him, and know what he doeth?
52 They answered and said unto him, Art thou also of Galilee? Search, and look: for out of Galilee ariseth no prophet.
53 And every man went unto his own house.

Sure enough, Jesus went to the appointed festival a bit late, possibly arriving there on the fourth day. He would thus miss most of the pilgrim cavalcades. He may have traveled via Samaria and missed the general traffic of the regular route. He had denied His family's rationale for going and had also chosen His own time as well. Some have identified His late arrival with Malachi's word: "Suddenly the Lord whom you seek will come to his temple" (3:1b, NEB).

1. It was soon evident that there was piled-up opposition to Jesus from the religious leaders. These included: *(a)* the chief priests, the Sadducees, whose area of concern was the Temple worship and revenues; *(b)* the elders, who were close to the ruling priests; *(c)* the Pharisees, who were the ecclesiastical lawyers and whose area of supervision was the synagogue. They were consequently closer to the people of their faith and were the popular leaders.

It was at the height of the festival that Jesus went up to the Temple and began to teach. He had timed His approach, but He was not timid. In fact, He came with a strong prophetic note. It was Calvin who observed in his writing, "We must always beware we do not for the sake of life lose the purpose of living."[4] Jesus took the offensive in His line of debate.

a. He affirmed His teaching was sound because it came from God who sent Him.

b. He insisted that His motive was pure, saying, "But if a man aims at the honour of him who sent him he is sincere, and there is nothing false in him" (18*b*, NEB).

c. He challenged them with, "Why do you seek to kill me?"

d. He insisted, "Whoever has the will to do the will of God shall know whether my teaching comes from him or is merely my own" (17, NEB).

e. He pointed out that even under the Mosaic law it was legal to circumcise on the Sabbath Day. He argued then, Why couldn't He do good, like healing, on the Sabbath Day?

f. His summary appeal was: "Do not judge superficially, but be just in your judgments" (24, NEB).

2. It is probably true that there is more piled up animosity in chapters 7 and 8 than in any other two chapters in the four accounts of the gospel. The moral and spiritual climate around Jesus was cynical and tinctured with bitterness.

The general view of the Jews was a mixture of astonishment and occasional admiration. It was a case of an uncredited teacher putting the credited ones on the defensive. Jesus' penetration was frequently unanswerable. He usually reached for the heart of the given issue.

3. They even sent a band of Temple police to arrest Him (because of His popularity), but they returned without their prisoner. (This was probably six months before Judas' betrayal.) In explanation the officers exclaimed: "No man ever spoke like this man!" Then Nicodemus (who belonged to the Sanhedrin) asked seriously, "Does our law permit us to pass judgment on a man unless we have first given him a hearing and learned the facts?" (51, NEB). But the only reply that the chief priests could muster was *(argumentum ad hominum,* or argument to the man), "Are you a Galilean too?"

Jesus actually started about this time to prepare His apostles for the Cross that was rising up before Him. His mission would soon be thrust into their hands.

In reviewing the above, it seems fitting to lift up the critical verse (17) as an index for discovering the truth of God; "Whoever has the will to do the will of God shall know whether my teaching comes from him or is merely my own" (NEB).

(See appendix for a sermon outline on this passage.)

Standing on the promises that cannot fail!
When the howling storms of doubt and fear assail,
By the living Word of God I shall prevail,
Standing on the promises of God.

Standing on the promises of Christ, the Lord,
Bound to Him eternally by love's strong cord,
Overcoming daily with the Spirit's Sword,
Standing on the promises of God.

Promise of the Holy Spirit's Coming

John 7:37-44

37 In the last day, that great day of the feast, Jesus stood and cried, saying, If any man thirst, let him come unto me, and drink.
38 He that believeth on me, as the scripture hath said, out of his belly shall flow rivers of living water.
39 (But this spake he of the Spirit, which they that believe on him should receive: for the Holy Ghost was not yet given; because that Jesus was not yet glorified.)
40 Many of the people therefore, when they heard this saying, said, Of a truth this is the Prophet.
41 Others said, This is the Christ. But some said, Shall Christ come out of Galilee?
42 Hath not the scripture said, That Christ cometh of the seed of David, and out of the town of Bethlehem, where David was?
43 So there was a division among the people because of him.
44 And some of them would have taken him; but no man laid hands on him.

The Feast of Tabernacles was probably the outstanding festal occasion in Israel. It was a national and religious event, and Jerusalem and the Temple constituted the center of the celebration. The people stayed in leafy temporary booths placed all over the city and outlying places, in the courts of houses and on the roofs. This was to honor God for His shelter and provision during their wanderings in the wilderness. It reminded them of their national history.

It was also held in the fall of the year, so the festival also carried the tone of thanksgiving for the harvest of the current year.

1. One of the rituals included the daily drawing of water from the Pool of Siloam and from there priests carried the water in golden vessels and then poured it out in an open container. Pipes carried this water to the altar. As they carried the water, the priests sang from Isaiah, "With joy shall ye draw water out of the wells of salvation" (12:3).

The feast originally lasted seven days, but it was extended to eight days. This was the final and great day. It was a day of holy convocation and was climactic, for it was the conclusion of the Feast of Tabernacles and of the festal year. It was on this last day that Jesus spoke His prophetic message, for He was no longer seated to teach; He stood to proclaim. John declares He cried aloud: "If any one thirst, let him come to me and drink. He who believes in me, as the scripture has said, 'Out of his heart shall flow rivers of living water'" (37-38, RSV).

2. John then gives us the exegesis or interpretation so we are not left to puzzle it out by ourselves. "Now this he said about the Spirit, which those who believed him were to receive; for as yet the Spirit had not been given, because Jesus was not yet glorified" (39, RSV).

The reaction to this message was mixed. Some said, "This is really the prophet" (who was to come); others said, "This is the Christ" (Messiah). Still others argued that the Christ (the Anointed One) could not come out of Galilee. Still another group wanted to arrest Him, "but no one laid hands on him" (40-44).

(See appendix for a sermon outline on John 7:37-39.)

JOHN 8

The Woman Taken in Adultery

John 8:1-11

1 Jesus went unto the mount of Olives.
2 And early in the morning he came again into the temple, and all the people came unto him; and he sat down, and taught them.
3 And the scribes and Pharisees brought unto him a woman taken in adultery; and when they had set her in the midst,
4 They say unto him, Master, this woman was taken in adultery, in the very act.
5 Now Moses in the law commanded us, that such should be stoned: but what sayest thou?
6 This they said, tempting him, that they might have to accuse him. But Jesus stooped down, and with his finger wrote on the ground, as though he heard them not.
7 So when they continued asking him, he lifted up himself, and said unto them, He that is without sin among you, let him first cast a stone at her.
8 And again he stooped down, and wrote on the ground.

9 And they which heard it, being convicted by their own conscience, went out one by one, beginning at the eldest, even unto the last: and Jesus was left alone, and the woman standing in the midst.

10 When Jesus had lifted up himself, and saw none but the woman, he said unto her, Woman, where are those thine accusers? hath no man condemned thee?

11 She said, No man, Lord. And Jesus said unto her, Neither do I condemn thee: go, and sin no more.

1. The confrontation of Jesus by the group of scribes and Pharisees concerning the woman taken in adultery was a rather indelicate affair. Those men made the woman stand in front while they presented their propositional question to Jesus. They reminded Him of the Mosaic law and the accompanying penalty of death by stoning. They reported that she had "been caught in the very act of adultery" (4, NEB). Then their question was, "What do you say about it?"

The truth was, capital punishment by the Jews was illegal under Roman rule, so that their stoning was to that extent lynch law. However, the Roman governors sometimes winked at the religious regulations and practices of the Jews.

2. Jesus' reply was an eloquent silence, but not heartless. He wrote in the dust with His finger while the men looked on. They continued to press their question, for they were sure they had Him on the horns of a dilemma. Presently He sat up straight and said to them, "Let him who is without sin among you cast the first stone at her" (7, RSV). Then Jesus resumed His finger-writing in the dust. When it dawned on the accusers where they stood, they left one by one, beginning at the eldest. J. Campbell Morgan suggests, "I prefer to think that the oldest man went first, because he had the most sense."[5]

Then Jesus turned to the accused and said to her, "'Woman, where are they? Has no one condemned thee?' She said, 'No one, Lord.' And Jesus said, 'Neither do I condemn you; go, and do not sin again'" (10-11, NEB). She was acquitted. But where was the man?

3. Some of the older manuscripts do not contain this story. However, it is not difficult for us to receive this tradition with the climate of chapters seven and eight in John's Gospel. Also, it was very difficult for evil men to ultimately corner Him who knew no sin!

Jesus the Light of the World

John 8:12-20

> 12 Then spake Jesus again unto them, saying, I am the light of the world: he that followeth me shall not walk in darkness, but shall have the light of life.
> 13 The Pharisees therefore said unto him, Thou bearest record of thyself; thy record is not true.
> 14 Jesus answered and said unto them, Though I bear record of myself, yet my record is true: for I know whence I came, and whither I go; but ye cannot tell whence I come, and whither I go.
> 15 Ye judge after the flesh; I judge no man.
> 16 And yet if I judge, my judgment is true: for I am not alone, but I and the Father that sent me.
> 17 It is also written in your law, that the testimony of two men is true.
> 18 I am one that bear witness of myself, and the Father that sent me beareth witness of me.
> 19 Then said they unto him, Where is thy Father? Jesus answered, Ye neither know me, nor my Father: if ye had known me, ye should have known my Father also.
> 20 These words spake Jesus in the treasury, as he taught in the temple: and no man laid hands on him; for his hour was not yet come.

In identifying himself as "The Light of the World," we have another of Jesus' famous "I Am"s. These identify both Jesus' character and His mission. His light flows from His life. John had stated this early in his Prologue: "In him was life, and the life was the light of men" (1:4, RSV). But the mission of light was to shine in darkness. Also here Jesus follows it up with the application, "No follower of mine shall wander in the dark; he shall have the light of life" (12, NEB).

1. The scene of our lesson is probably the day following the climactic day of the Feast of Tabernacles. Jesus is in the Court of the Women (where they could attend along with the men), and it was here that the great golden candle-

sticks had been lit during the feast, so it was especially appropriate that Jesus should relate himself to light.

The treasury was in the Court of the Women. It was here that there were also placed 13 trumpet-shaped collection boxes, and each box had an appropriate description showing the purported use of each box. At least, they did not shut the women off from giving, even as Jesus had witnessed! (See Mark 12:41-44.)

2. The light comes from life, but it also issues in life. The supreme evidence for light is that it shines. Darkness cannot overcome it. It also affords the tone of life. Jesus warned earlier that the real struggle and source of unbelief was a bad heart and evil living! "Here lies the test: the light has come into the world, but men preferred darkness to light because their deeds were evil. Bad men all hate the light and avoid it, for fear their practices should be shown up. The honest man comes to the light so that it may be clearly seen that God is in all he does" (3:19-21, NEB).

3. There is a sense in which Calvary (that was shrouded so much with darkness) was actually the place where the "eternal flame" of Christ's light was lit, and it still shines.

P. P. Bliss's hymn is appropriate here:

No darkness have we who in Jesus abide;
The Light of the world is Jesus.
We walk in the Light when we follow our Guide;
The Light of the world is Jesus.

No need of the sunlight in heaven we're told;
The Light of the World is Jesus.
The Lamb is the Light in the city of gold;
The Light of the world is Jesus.

Come to the Light; 'tis shining for thee.
Sweetly the Light has dawned upon me.
Once I was blind, but now I can see.
The Light of the world is Jesus.

Further Teaching of Jesus About Who He Is

John 8:21-59

21 Then said Jesus again unto them, I go my way, and ye shall seek me, and shall die in your sins: whither I go, ye cannot come.

22 Then said the Jews, Will he kill himself? because he saith, Whither I go, ye cannot come.

23 And he said unto them, Ye are from beneath; I am from above: ye are of this world; I am not of this world.

24 I said therefore unto you, that ye shall die in your sins: for if ye believe not that I am he, ye shall die in your sins.

25 Then said they unto him, Who art thou? And Jesus saith unto them, Even the same that I said unto you from the beginning.

26 I have many things to say and to judge of you: but he that sent me is true; and I speak to the world those things which I have heard of him.

27 They understood not that he spake to them of the Father.

28 Then said Jesus unto them, When ye have lifted up the Son of man, then shall ye know that I am he, and that I do nothing of myself; but as my Father hath taught me, I speak these things.

29 And he that sent me is with me: the Father hath not left me alone; for I do always those things that please him.

30 As he spake these words, many believed on him.

31 Then said Jesus to those Jews which believed on him, If ye continue in my word, then are ye my disciples indeed;

32 And ye shall know the truth, and the truth shall make you free.

33 They answered him, We be Abraham's seed, and were never in bondage to any man: how sayest thou, Ye shall be made free?

34 Jesus answered them, Verily, verily, I say unto you, Whosoever committeth sin is the servant of sin.

35 And the servant abideth not in the house for ever: but the Son abideth ever.

36 If the Son therefore shall make you free, ye shall be free indeed.

37 I know that ye are Abraham's seed; but ye seek to kill me, because my word hath no place in you.

38 I speak that which I have seen with my Father: and ye do that which ye have seen with your father.

39 They answered and said unto him, Abraham is our father. Jesus saith unto them, If ye were Abraham's children, ye would do the works of Abraham.

40 But now ye seek to kill me, a man that hath told you the truth, which I have heard of God: this did not Abraham.

41 Ye do the deeds of your father. Then said they to him, We be not born of fornication; we have one Father, even God.

42 Jesus said unto them, If God were your Father, ye would love me: for I proceeded forth and came from God; neither came I of myself, but he sent me.

43 Why do ye not understand my speech? even because ye cannot hear my word.

44 Ye are of your father the devil, and the lusts of your father ye will do. He was a murderer from the beginning, and abode not in the truth, because there is no truth in him. When he speaketh a lie, he speaketh of his own: for he is a liar, and the father of it.

45 And because I tell you the truth, ye believe me not.

46 Which of you convinceth me of sin? And if I say the truth, why do ye not believe me?

47 He that is of God heareth God's words: ye therefore hear them not, because ye are not of God.

48 Then answered the Jews, and said unto him, Say we not well that thou art a Samaritan, and hast a devil?

49 Jesus answered, I have not a devil; but I honour my Father, and ye do dishonour me.

50 And I seek not mine own glory: there is one that seeketh and judgeth.

51 Verily, verily, I say unto you, If a man keep my saying, he shall never see death.

52 Then said the Jews unto him, Now we know that thou hast a devil. Abraham is dead, and the prophets; and thou sayest, If a man keep my saying, he shall never taste of death.

53 Art thou greater than our father Abraham, which is dead? and the prophets are dead: whom makest thou thyself?

54 Jesus answered, If I honour myself, my honour is nothing: it is my Father that honoureth me; of whom ye say, that he is your God:

55 Yet ye have not known him; but I know him: and if I should say, I know him not, I shall be a liar like unto you: but I know him, and keep his saying.

56 Your father Abraham rejoiced to see my day: and he saw it, and was glad.

57 Then said the Jews unto him, Thou art not yet fifty years old, and hast thou seen Abraham?

58 Jesus said unto them, Verily, verily, I say unto you, Before Abraham was, I am.

59 Then took they up stones to cast at him: but Jesus hid himself, and went out of the temple, going through the midst of them, and so passed by.

The entrenched opposition of the leading Jews to Jesus is increasingly clear in this passage. Also the clash is highlighted as Jesus reveals the true source of their cross-purposes.

1. Twice He tells them that they will die in their sins, but in the second instance He enumerates why: "Unless you believe that I am he" (21, 24, RSV).

2. Jesus argues that they are not on the same level or approach concerning the heart of the issues discussed. Constantly Jesus shows that His point of view comes from the Father, while theirs is an earthly or worldly approach or philosophy. He insists twice that they are the slaves of sin, because they are in bondage to it.

3. Also twice He faces them with the fact that they are bent on killing Him. He explains their murderous intentions, based on His teaching which they had rejected. (See 8:37 and 40, NEB.) He insists that God is the true source of His teaching, but He acknowledges that His teaching was making no headway with them.

4. Jesus also explains the clash based on their conflicting sources (His and theirs); hence no reconciliation. Jesus states this clearly and sharply since His teaching came from God, theirs came from the devil or Satan. He underscores the moral unreliability of Satan saying, "He was a murderer from the beginning, and has nothing to do with the truth, because there is no truth in him. When he lies, he speaks according to his own nature, for he is a liar and the father of lies" (44b, RSV). He calls God His father and the devil theirs.

5. He insists that if they loved God, they would love Him, but they demurred. Jesus infers that their distance from God is a moral distance. In one instance when they had accused Him of being demon possessed, He answered with, "I have not a demon; but I honor my Father, and you dishonor me" (49, RSV).

All of this was heavy artillery, and at short range! John acknowledges that sometimes they did not know what He meant (27, RSV).

6. On the positive side Jesus testifies that His chief motivation and mode of operation is essentially to please His Father. It is a way of life with Him, and the Father, in turn, affords Him His unfailing presence. The truth is, His total mission is an appointment by the Father. Jesus declares: "I do nothing on my own authority but speak thus as the Father taught me. And he who sent me is with me; he has not left me alone, for I always do what is pleasing to him" (28b-29, RSV).

7. What a code for moral conduct and radiant living! This

was the reverse of self-willing and self-centeredness; it was the freedom of moral likeness and better than a memorized code of rules. His Father's slightest hint carried love's imperative with Him. But this was also the Son's delight. Jowett expresses it well: "Sin is not a question of breaking God's law; it is a question of breaking God's heart."[6] Perhaps it is both; they are in harmony.

Faber writes of the breadth of God's mercy:

For the love of God is broader
Than the measure of man's mind;
And the heart of the Eternal
Is most wonderfully kind.

If our love were but more simple,
We should take Him at His word;
And our lives would be all sunshine
In the sweetness of the Lord.

8. The climax of this story was actually anticlimactic. When Jesus told them, "In every truth I tell you, before Abraham was born, I am," immediately "they picked up stones to throw at him, but Jesus was not to be seen; and he left the temple" (58, NEB). When the writer was a boy visiting his relatives in north Ireland years ago, he learned to call the "stone piles" "Irish confetti." But the Jews learned this deadly game long ago. It was mob rule—lynch law, at best. It was lawlessness carried out in the name of the law. That was how Stephen—a layman, the first recorded, post-Pentecost martyr—met his death. But his witness probably "stung" one of the most zealous and more intelligent men on the other side, who had agreed silently with the lawlessness just committed. He, too, finally gave in and knelt to pray, and years afterwards joined the martyrs' noble band.

JOHN 9

A Blind Beggar Receives His Sight: The Sixth Sign

John 9:1-41

1 And as Jesus passed by, he saw a man which was blind from his birth.

2 And his disciples asked him, saying, Master, who did sin, this man, or his parents, that he was born blind?

3 Jesus answered, Neither hath this man sinned, nor his parents: but that the works of God should be made manifest in him.

4 I must work the works of him that sent me, while it is day: the night cometh, when no man can work.

5 As long as I am in the world, I am the light of the world.

6 When he had thus spoken, he spat on the ground, and made clay of the spittle, and he anointed the eyes of the blind man with the clay,

7 And said unto him, Go, wash in the pool of Siloam, (Which is by interpretation, Sent.) He went his way therefore, and washed, and came seeing.

8 The neighbours therefore, and they which before had seen him that he was blind, said, Is not this he that sat and begged?

9 Some said, This is he: others said, He is like him: but he said, I am he.

10 Therefore said they unto him, How were thine eyes opened?

11 He answered and said, A man that is called Jesus made clay, and anointed mine eyes, and said unto me, Go to the pool of Siloam, and wash: and I went and washed, and I received sight.

12 Then said they unto him, Where is he? He said, I know not.

13 They brought to the Pharisees him that aforetime was blind.

14 And it was the sabbath day when Jesus made the clay, and opened his eyes.

15 Then again the Pharisees also asked him how he had received his sight. He said unto them, He put clay upon mine eyes, and I washed, and do see.

16 Therefore said some of the Pharisees, This man is not of God, because he keepeth not the sabbath day. Others said, How can a man that is a sinner do such miracles? And there was a division among them.

17 They say unto the blind man again, What sayest thou of him, that he hath opened thine eyes? He said, He is a prophet.

18 But the Jews did not believe concerning him, that he had been blind, and received his sight, until they called the parents of him that had received his sight.

19 And they asked them, saying, Is this your son, who ye say was born blind? how then doth he now see?

20 His parents answered them and said, We know that this is our son, and that he was born blind:

21 But by what means he now seeth, we know not; or who hath opened his eyes, we know not: he is of age; ask him: he shall speak for himself.

22 These words spake his parents, because they feared the Jews: for the Jews had agreed already, that if any man did confess that he was Christ, he should be put out of the synagogue.

23 Therefore said his parents, He is of age; ask him.

24 Then again called they the man that was blind, and said unto him, Give God the praise: we know that this man is a sinner.

25 He answered and said, Whether he be a sinner or no, I know not: one thing I know, that, whereas I was blind, now I see.

26 Then said they to him again, What did he to thee? how opened he thine eyes?

27 He answered them, I have told you already, and ye did not hear: wherefore would ye hear it again? will ye also be his disciples?

28 Then they reviled him, and said, Thou art his disciple; but we are Moses' disciples.

29 We know that God spake unto Moses: as for this fellow, we know not from whence he is.

30 The man answered and said unto them, Why herein is a marvellous thing, that ye know not from whence he is, and yet he hath opened mine eyes.

31 Now we know that God heareth not sinners: but if any man be a worshipper of God, and doeth his will, him he heareth.

32 Since the world began was it not heard that any man opened the eyes of one that was born blind.

33 If this man were not of God, he could do nothing.

34 They answered and said unto him, Thou wast altogether born in sins, and dost thou teach us? And they cast him out.

35 Jesus heard that they had cast him out; and when he had found him, he said unto him, Dost thou believe on the Son of God?

36 He answered and said, Who is he, Lord, that I might believe on him?

37 And Jesus said unto him, Thou hast both seen him, and it is he that talketh with thee.

38 And he said, Lord, I believe. And he worshipped him.

39 And Jesus said, For judgment I am come into this world, that they which see not might see; and that they which see might be made blind.

40 And some of the Pharisees which were with him heard these words, and said unto him, Are we blind also?

41 Jesus said unto them, If ye were blind, ye should have no sin: but now ye say, We see; therefore your sin remaineth.

This story of the man who was healed of congenital blindness is the only such miracle recorded in the New Testament. So far as we know, there are no Old Testament accounts of giving sight to the blind.

This healing came at a time when Jesus' accumulating "signs" or miracles had given Him an unusual following. Conversely, the leaders of Jewry had also intensified their opposition until they had already begun to plot Jesus' death.

1. *The Healing.* In this scene again, Jesus does not plan

a prime-time setting for the miracle. He met the man "en route," as "he [Jesus] went on his way" (9:1, NEB). Similarly, the method employed was simple, but it required a response from the man. Jesus was not there when the cure was effected; neither did He meet the man on his immediate return home.

Among His own inner circle, the question arose about the real cause or source of this man's blindness, especially whether or not it was brought about by sin. The disciples asked, "Rabbi, who sinned, this man or his parents? Why was he born blind?" Jesus answered: "It is not that this man or his parents sinned . . . he was born blind that God's power might be displayed in curing him. . . . We must carry on the work of him who sent me; night comes, when no one can work. While I am in the world I am the light of the world" (9:2-5, NEB). Jesus had a new sense of urgency on Him at this time. Also He had begun to prepare His disciples and especially the apostles for the coming Cross that was looming up before Him.

Jesus had evidently stopped beside the blind man by now and had made a paste of mud or clay with spittle. Then He anointed the eyes of the blind beggar with the newly formed "mud-pack" and said, "Go and wash in the pool of Siloam." (The name Siloam really means "sent.") At least, the man went as he was told, washed as instructed, "and when he returned he could see" (7, NEB).

What a scene! What if that had been you or me? Fancy looking up his parents, seeing his friends, and taking a look at the sun and the whole countryside round about him—all for the first time in his life! What an explosion of joy and what a sense of deliverance must have overwhelmed him! Surely he would want everybody to be glad with him! This was the day of his life he would never forget. We could fancy he would soon throw away his beggar's cup. The world was wide open to him now for the first time. He could learn to read and write and find a useful occupation. Not much therapy for the blind in his day, to be sure.

2. *The Neighbors Respond.* Now the man whose sight was given to him was on his own. His neighbors who knew him when he was led about by someone could not believe their eyes. Those who had known him also as a beggar now asked, "Is not this the man who used to sit and beg?" Some said, "Yes, that's the one." Others answered, "No, but he looks like him." The man himself put in the decisive word, "I am the man," and his tone carried assurance with it. Next they asked him, "How were your eyes opened?" He replied, "The man called Jesus made a paste and smeared my eyes with it, and told me to go to Siloam and wash. I went and washed, and gained my sight." Then they asked, "Where is he?" He replied simply, "I don't know," for he had lost track of Jesus since He sent him to the Pool of Siloam (8-12).

3. *The Pharisees Move in on the Scene.* The excited people kept talking and led the healed man to the Pharisees. Now the tone is not so friendly and the discussion is more heated. The Pharisees were almost pugnacious in their approach. But the healed man still had a glow on his countenance. Augustine commented on it long ago: "Endowed with sight, he becomes a confessor. That blind man makes a confession and the heart of the wicked was troubled; for they had not in their hearts what he had now in his countenance."[7]

John reminds us that this healing was done on the Sabbath day, and that made a difference to these Pharisees. They asked the man all over again by what means he had received his sight. He said, "He put clay on my eyes, and I washed, and I see" (15). Some of the Pharisees then volunteered, "This fellow is no man of God; he does not keep the Sabbath." Others of them asked, "How could such signs come from a sinful man?" (16). So the Pharisees themselves were divided. Then they continued to question the man and put him on the spot saying, "What have you to say about him? It was your eyes he opened" (17, NEB). The man replied simply, "He is a prophet."

Then the Pharisees doubted the facts recounted to them and summoned the man's parents to verify or correct the story given. This group that was checking up could have been one of the two smaller synagogue courts that cared for minor problems. They asked the parents (who seemed to be nervous from the start): (1) Is this man your son? (2) Do you say he was born blind? (3) How is it that he now sees?

The parents evidently had heard the word that had gone out from the authorities to the effect that if anyone acknowledged that this Jesus was the Christ (Messiah), he should be banned from the synagogue. The parents readily confessed the identity of their son and that he was born blind. But when it came to his healing they said, "He is of age; ask him."

4. *Excommunicated!* Then they turned to the healed man again. This time they said, "Give God the glory." This really meant in current legal practice, "Tell the truth." They added, "We know that this fellow is a sinner." The man replied: "Whether or not he is a sinner, I do not know. All I know is this: once I was blind, now I can see" (25, NEB). They pressed him with, "How did he open your eyes?" "I have told you already," he retorted, "but you took no notice. Why do you want to hear it again? Do you also want to become his disciples?" (26-27, NEB). Then his interrogators became abusive, for the man's last replies contained a sting in them. His years of begging evidently had not cancelled his self-esteem; and besides, everything looked different to him now since he had gained his eyesight.

The Pharisees replied that they followed Moses. They insisted, "We know that God spoke to Moses, but as for this fellow, we do not know where he comes from" (29, NEB). Again the healed man answered them with some vigor, "What an extraordinary thing! Here is a man who has opened my eyes, yet you do not know where he comes from!" (30, NEB). Then he added with confidence, "If that man had not come from God he could have done nothing" (33, NEB). He had learned this evidently as a blind boy in the synagogue. With added bitterness, they retorted, "Who are you to give us lessons, born and bred in sin as you are?" (34, NEB). They thus flung the usual taunt that his previous blindness had come from his own or his parents' sins. The inevitable happened; "They expelled him from the synagogue" (34, NEB). The roof had fallen in on him!

5. *Something Good Happens.* Then something good happened to the man they had excommunicated. When Jesus learned what the Pharisees had done, He sought for the man and asked him, "Do you believe in the Son of Man?" He answered anxiously, "And who is he, sir, that I may believe in him?" Jesus said to him, "You have seen him, and he it is who speaks to you." At that the man said, "Lord, I believe." The record concludes with, "And he worshiped him" (35-38, RSV).

Chrysostom summarized this picture long ago: "The Jews cast him out from the Temple, and the Lord of the Temple found him."[8] In more recent years Jowett observed in the same vein, "The man who had received his sight was cast out, but on the threshold he met his Lord."[9] What a Lord! What a man! What a day!

Morgan observes, "Jesus received this man's worship. In that moment the new economy was born."[10] This was the only kind of kingdom that was worth dying for.

> *Jesus calls us from the worship*
> *Of this vain world's golden store,*
> *From each idol that would keep us,*
> *Saying, "Christian, love Me more."*
>
> *Jesus calls us. By Thy mercies,*
> *Saviour, may we hear Thy call,*
> *Give our hearts to Thy obedience,*
> *Serve and love Thee best of all.*

Parable of the Shepherd

John 10:1-21

1 Verily, verily, I say unto you, He that entereth not by the door into the sheepfold, but climbeth up some other way, the same is a thief and a robber.

2 But he that entereth in by the door is the shepherd of the sheep.

3 To him the porter openeth; and the sheep hear his voice: and he calleth his own sheep by name, and leadeth them out.

4 And when he putteth forth his own sheep, he goeth before them, and the sheep follow him: for they know his voice.

5 And a stranger will they not follow, but will flee from him: for they know not the voice of strangers.

6 This parable spake Jesus unto them: but they understood not what things they were which he spake unto them.

7 Then said Jesus unto them again, Verily, verily, I say unto you, I am the door of the sheep.

8 All that ever came before me are thieves and robbers: but the sheep did not hear them.

9 I am the door: by me if any man enter in, he shall be saved, and shall go in and out, and find pasture.

10 The thief cometh not, but for to steal, and to kill, and to destroy: I am come that they might have life, and that they might have it more abundantly.

11 I am the good shepherd: the good shepherd giveth his life for the sheep.

12 But he that is an hireling, and not the shepherd, whose own the sheep are not, seeth the wolf coming, and leaveth the sheep, and fleeth: and the wolf catcheth them, and scattereth the sheep.

13 The hireling fleeth, because he is an hireling, and careth not for the sheep.

14 I am the good shepherd, and know my sheep, and am known of mine.

15 As the Father knoweth me, even so know I the Father: and I lay down my life for the sheep.

16 And other sheep I have, which are not of this fold: them also I must bring, and they shall hear my voice; and there shall be one fold, and one shepherd.

17 Therefore doth my Father love me, because I lay down my life, that I might take it again.

18 No man taketh it from me, but I lay it down of myself. I have power to lay it down, and I have power to take it again. This commandment have I received of my Father.

19 There was a division therefore again among the Jews for these sayings.

20 And many of them said, He hath a devil, and is mad; why hear ye him?

21 Others said, These are not the words of him that hath a devil. Can a devil open the eyes of the blind?

The parable of the Shepherd follows sometime after the healing of the blind beggar. It opens with that characteristic note of certainty: "Verily, verily," which means, "Amen, amen!" Jesus identifies himself as "The Good Shepherd," or "The Shepherd Good."

1. This was a familiar approach to the care of souls in the Old Testament, especially in the Psalms and in the Prophets. An example would be the best known, and probably the best loved psalm, the 23rd. It deals with evil and sin in the world including—want, trouble, sorrow, death, strife, and enemies. But the key to deliverance is in the opening line, "The Lord is my shepherd." Jesus seems to say, "I am that good Shepherd that men need."

Also, the compassionate Shepherd who was to come had been prophesied by Isaiah. He wrote of His majestic tenderness: "Behold your God! . . . He will lead his flock like a shepherd, he will gather the lambs in his arms, and he will carry them in his bosom, and gently lead those that are with young" (40:9*b*, 11, NEB). Jesus himself is the fulfillment of that prophetic expectation!

Conversely, the prophet Ezekiel gave the divine condemnation upon the careless and selfish shepherds in his day: "Thus saith the Lord God: Ho, shepherds of Israel who have been feeding yourselves! Should not shepherds feed the sheep? You eat the fat, you clothe yourselves with the wool, you slaughter the fatlings; you do not feed the sheep. The weak you have not strengthened, the sick you have not healed, the crippled you have not bound up, the strayed you have not brought back, the lost you have not sought, and with force and harshness you have ruled them" (34:2*b*-5, RSV). It was contemporaries such as these that Jesus called hirelings, even thieves and robbers, and some of them He depicted as wolves.

2. Jesus stands in sweet contrast to this dark picture. His own heart and mission, in complete harmony with the Father, make Him the Shepherd Good. He even dares to lay down His own life for the sheep, and the Father loves

Him all the more for this compassion (17). But He is careful to point out that His death (to come) would not be simply the result of the command or caprice of wicked men. It was the outcome of His own accord with His Father's will (18). He insisted, "I have power to lay it down, and I have power to take it again; this commandment [charge] I have received from my Father" (18*b*).

This symbolism of the Good Shepherd and His sheep is a familiar one in Palestine, and Jesus made the application both practical and penetrating. It begins with a personal relation. He actually begins by identifying himself as the door of the sheep. This is a mixed figure, but there is an admixture of care and provision in this combination.

3. The usual enclosure for the sheep at nighttime could be near the shepherd's home, or it could be an appointed place where four walls would mark their shelter for the night. One of the walls had an opening and that is where the sheep entered in or departed from. There was no door as such, so it could not be barred or locked against marauders, either men or beasts. It was the shepherd himself who guarded the open place with his own stretched out body, and their defense was his life. He slept at the open place and his very body became the door.

It is also through the assistance of the shepherd that the sheep secure nourishment. He is their way of life. It is by him they go in and out and find pasture. He is the supreme authority for the access to their lives. He leads, he directs; he never drives. He has a sensitive awareness that they are following him. He can never divorce himself from this responsibility. No wolf can snatch them out of his care. He has the patience of strength and a peculiar discernment in his understanding. He waits for their fears to dispel.

There is also a very personal identity for all who follow the Shepherd Good. He calls and they recognize His voice. They learn to know Him by His prohibitions as well as His provisions. The shepherd does make His demands and His sheep learn to trust His judgment. His followers are known one by one. His voice is distinguishable to them. His love is hard to simulate. His goodness cannot be duplicated. Personal needs are as real as faces. He cares enough to know each one personally.

Jesus insisted He was the only one who afforded them access to the Father. He also promised that "other sheep" would follow His present flock. These would become one fellowship, for they all would have the same Good Shepherd.

4. William Barclay relates a lovely Jewish legend concerning Moses, for he too was a shepherd. It is an imaginative and reverent conjecture on why Moses was chosen as the leader of the people of God. "When Moses was feeding the sheep of his father-in-law in the wilderness, a young kid ran away. Moses followed it until it reached a ravine, where it found a well from which to drink. When Moses came up to it, he said: 'I did not know that you ran away because you were thirsty. Now you must be weary.' So he took the kid on his shoulders and carried it back. Then God said, 'Because you have shown pity in leading back one of a flock belonging to a man, you shall lead my flock, Israel.'"[11]

It was Stephen, that lay preacher and first recorded martyr, who reminded us that "Moses was educated in all wisdom of the Egyptians, and was mighty in words and in deeds" (Acts 7:22, John Wesley's translation). He was then 40 years old, but God led him into 40 years of post graduate studies and experience in the wilderness as a shepherd to prepare him for 40 years of full-time service in bringing His people from longtime slavery to the land of promise.

No wonder that here Jesus should identify himself as the Good Shepherd!

At the close of this climactic discourse, many of them said, "He is possessed, he is raving, why listen to him?"

Others said, "Could an evil spirit open blind men's eyes?"
(20-21, NEB).

Here is another old hymn for our prayer today.

> *Savior, like a shepherd lead us;*
> *Much we need Thy tender care.*
> *In Thy pleasant pastures feed us;*
> *For our use Thy folds prepare.*
> *Blessed Jesus, blessed Jesus!*
> *Thou hast bought us; Thine we are.*
>
> *Thou hast promised to receive us,*
> *Poor and sinful tho' we be;*
> *Thou hast mercy to relieve us,*
> *Grace to cleanse, and power to free*
> *Blessed Jesus, blessed Jesus!*
> *We will early turn to Thee.*
>
> *We are thine, do Thou befriend us;*
> *Be the Guardian of our way.*
> *Keep Thy flock; from sin defend us;*
> *Seek us when we go astray.*
> *Blessed Jesus, blessed Jesus!*
> *Hear, O hear us, when we pray.*
>
> —DOROTHY A. THRUPP

At the Feast of Dedication

John 10:22-42

22 And it was at Jerusalem the feast of the dedication, and it was winter.

23 And Jesus walked in the temple in Solomon's porch.

24 Then came the Jews round about him, and said unto him, How long dost thou make us to doubt? If thou be the Christ, tell us plainly.

25 Jesus answered them, I told you, and ye believed not: the works that I do in my Father's name, they bear witness of me.

26 But ye believe not, because ye are not of my sheep, as I said unto you.

27 My sheep hear my voice, and I know them, and they follow me:

28 And I give unto them eternal life; and they shall never perish, neither shall any man pluck them out of my hand.

29 My Father, which gave them me, is greater than all; and no man is able to pluck them out of my Father's hand.

30 I and my Father are one.

31 Then the Jews took up stones again to stone him.

32 Jesus answered them, Many good works have I shewed you from my Father; for which of those works do ye stone me?

33 The Jews answered him, saying, For a good work we stone thee not; but for blasphemy; and because that thou, being a man, makest thyself God.

34 Jesus answered them, Is it not written in your law, I said, Ye are gods?

35 If he called them gods, unto whom the word of God came, and the scripture cannot be broken;

36 Say ye of him, whom the Father hath sanctified, and sent into the world, Thou blasphemest; because I said, I am the Son of God?

37 If I do not the works of my Father, believe me not.

38 But if I do, though ye believe not me, believe the works: that ye may know, and believe, that the Father is in me, and I in him.

39 Therefore they sought again to take him: but he escaped out of their hand,

40 And went away again beyond Jordan into the place where John at first baptized; and there he abode.

41 And many resorted unto him, and said, John did no miracle: but all things that John spake of this man were true.

42 And many believed on him there.

The Feast of Dedication was a relatively recent festival. It commemorated the rededication of the Temple by Judas Maccabaeus in 165 B.C., having been profaned earlier by the pagan king, Antiochus Epiphanes. It was sometimes identified technically as the Festival of Hanukkah, and it could be observed in any suitable place. In the popular sense, it was commonly called the Feast of Lights.

The feast was held at the time of the winter solstice, which would bring it close to our Christmas season. It lasted eight days. Morris reminds us that "it was the last great deliverance that the Jews had known and therefore it must have been in men's minds a symbol of their hope that God would again deliver His people."[12]

1. How fitting that Jesus should elect to be in Jerusalem at this festival, for it was on this occasion that He had His last public ministry prior to His final return to finally face the Cross.

Jesus was walking in the Temple precincts in Solomon's cloister, a portico, in wintertime. The Jews gathered round about Him as though they had intentionally cornered Him and asked: "How long will you keep us in suspense? If you are the Christ, tell us plainly" (24b, RSV). Jesus' reply was that He had already told them, but they did not believe Him. Then He added quickly, "My deeds done in my Father's name are my credentials, but because you are not of my flock, you do not believe me" (25b-26, NEB). He knew that their concept of Messiahship was essentially political, while His was one of spiritual renewal, and redemptive. He continued, "My own sheep listen to my voice; I know them and they follow me. I give them eternal life and they shall never perish; no one will snatch them from my care" (27-28, NEB). Jesus concluded with the inner secret of himself and His mission: "My Father and I are one" (30).

2. That did it! Once again the surrounding Jews picked up stones to stone Him. With matchless poise Jesus countered with, "I have shown you many good works from the Father; for which of these do you stone me?" (32, RSV). But the Jews answered, "We stone you for no good work but for blasphemy; because you, being a man, make yourself God" (33, RSV). The debate continued and Jesus challenged them to test His life and service by the works performed. Jesus insisted that it was the Father who consecrated Him and gave Him His assignment, but the Jews only became more militant and provoked and tried once more to seize Him. "But he escaped from their clutches" (39, NEB). This same religious issue of blasphemy will be a critical one in the final trials (ecclesiastical and political) of Jesus.

3. Then Jesus withdrew again across the Jordan to the place where John the Baptist had identified Him as the Messiah (Christ). There, in despised Perea, many who had heard John and now heard Jesus for themselves testified, "All that he [John] said about this man was true" (41). The truth was John the Baptist would probably do more good among his own people after his head came off than he did with it on. In fact, when Jesus' fame had reached

Herod the Tetrarch earlier (after John's death), the governor said, "This is John the Baptist, he has risen from the dead" (Matt. 14:2, RSV).

The Raising of Lazarus: The Seventh Sign

John 11:1-53

1 Now a certain man was sick, named Lazarus, of Bethany, the town of Mary and her sister Martha.

2 (It was that Mary which anointed the Lord with ointment, and wiped his feet with her hair, whose brother Lazarus was sick.)

3 Therefore his sisters sent unto him, saying, Lord, behold, he whom thou lovest is sick.

4 When Jesus heard that, he said, This sickness is not unto death, but for the glory of God, that the Son of God might be glorified thereby.

5 Now Jesus loved Martha, and her sister, and Lazarus.

6 When he had heard therefore that he was sick, he abode two days still in the same place where he was.

7 Then after that saith he to his disciples, Let us go into Judaea again.

8 His disciples say unto him, Master, the Jews of late sought to stone thee; and goest thou thither again?

9 Jesus answered, Are there not twelve hours in the day? If any man walk in the day, he stumbleth not, because he seeth the light of this world.

10 But if a man walk in the night, he stumbleth, because there is no light in him.

11 These things said he: and after that he saith unto them, Our friend Lazarus sleepeth; but I go, that I may awake him out of sleep.

12 Then said his disciples, Lord, if he sleep, he shall do well.

13 Howbeit Jesus spake of his death: but they thought that he had spoken of taking of rest in sleep.

14 Then said Jesus unto them plainly, Lazarus is dead.

15 And I am glad for your sakes that I was not there, to the intent ye may believe; nevertheless let us go unto him.

16 Then said Thomas, which is called Didymus, unto his fellowdisciples, Let us also go, that we may die with him.

17 Then when Jesus came, he found that he had lain in the grave four days already.

18 Now Bethany was nigh unto Jerusalem, about fifteen furlongs off:

19 And many of the Jews came to Martha and Mary, to comfort them concerning their brother.

20 Then Martha, as soon as she heard that Jesus was coming, went and met him: but Mary sat still in the house.

21 Then said Martha unto Jesus, Lord, if thou hadst been here, my brother had not died.

22 But I know, that even now, whatsoever thou wilt ask of God, God will give it thee.

23 Jesus saith unto her, Thy brother shall rise again.

24 Martha saith unto him, I know that he shall rise again in the resurrection at the last day.

25 Jesus said unto her, I am the resurrection, and the life: he that believeth in me, though he were dead, yet shall he live:

26 And whosoever liveth and believeth in me shall never die. Believest thou this?

27 She saith unto him, Yea, Lord: I believe that thou art the Christ, the Son of God, which should come into the world.

28 And when she had so said, she went her way, and called Mary her sister secretly, saying, The Master is come, and calleth for thee.

29 As soon as she heard that, she arose quickly, and came unto him.

30 Now Jesus was not yet come into the town, but was in that place where Martha met him.

31 The Jews then which were with her in the house, and comforted her, when they saw Mary, that she rose up hastily and went out, followed her, saying, She goeth unto the grave to weep there.

32 Then when Mary was come where Jesus was, and saw him, she fell down at his feet, saying unto him, Lord, if thou hadst been here, my brother had not died.

33 When Jesus therefore saw her weeping, and the Jews also weeping which came with her, he groaned in the spirit, and was troubled,

34 And said, Where have ye laid him? They said unto him, Lord, come and see.

35 Jesus wept.

36 Then said the Jews, Behold how he loved him!

37 And some of them said, Could not this man, which opened the eyes of the blind, have caused that even this man should not have died?

38 Jesus therefore again groaning in himself cometh to the grave. It was a cave, and a stone lay upon it.

39 Jesus said, Take ye away the stone. Martha, the sister of him that was dead, saith unto him, Lord, by this time he stinketh: for he hath been dead four days.

40 Jesus saith unto her, Said I not unto thee, that, if thou wouldest believe, thou shouldest see the glory of God?

41 Then they took away the stone from the place where the dead was laid. And Jesus lifted up his eyes, and said, Father, I thank thee that thou hast heard me.

42 And I knew that thou hearest me always: but because of the people which stand by I said it, that they may believe that thou hast sent me.

43 And when he thus had spoken, he cried with a loud voice, Lazarus, come forth.

44 And he that was dead came forth, bound hand and foot with graveclothes: and his face was bound about with a napkin. Jesus saith unto them, Loose him, and let him go.

45 Then many of the Jews which came to Mary, and had seen the things which Jesus did, believed on him.

46 But some of them went their ways to the Pharisees, and told them what things Jesus had done.

47 Then gathered the chief priests and the Pharisees a council, and said, What do we? for this man doeth many miracles.

48 If we let him thus alone, all men will believe on him: and the Romans shall come and take away both our place and nation.

49 And one of them, named Caiaphas, being the high priest that same year, said unto them, Ye know nothing at all,
50 Nor consider that it is expedient for us, that one man should die for the people, and that the whole nation perish not.
51 And this spake he not of himself: but being high priest that year, he prophesied that Jesus should die for that nation;
52 And not for that nation only, but that also he should gather together in one the children of God that were scattered abroad.
53 Then from that day forth they took counsel together for to put him to death.

The raising of Lazarus from the dead is the seventh and climactic "sign" recorded in John's Gospel concerning Jesus' ministry of healing. John is the only evangelist who records this miracle. But there were two other reports of resurrection from the dead at the hands of our Lord. One was the restoration of the daughter of Jairus, the president of the synagogue in Capernaum. This was recorded by the three Synoptists. The other one was the raising of the son of the widow of Nain, en route to the burial place. Only Luke records this scene.

In the case of the restoration of the 12-year-old daughter of Jairus, she had just recently died before Jesus arrived. The widow's son was about to be buried and it was in the funeral procession that Jesus restored him. But Lazarus was dead for four days and properly buried and entombed when the unheard-of miracle was wrought.

In some respects this action of Jesus took place when He was running out of time. The Sadducees and Pharisees had tentatively agreed to work together against Jesus, but it was the rulers (the Sadducees) who took over in strategy plotting and with unrelenting and bitter determination. Redding observes that "the raising of Lazarus is the masterpiece of all the miracles of Christ and by far the most expensive—it cost Him His life."[13]

1. The setting for the sign and the leading characters involved included two sisters and a brother: Martha, Mary, and Lazarus. We judge that Martha was the older of the two women, for she seemed to be in charge of the household. Mary was the devout one who later on, but prior to His death, anointed her Lord with costly ointment. This

trio carried on in their own home, and when Jesus was with them, "He felt at home in their home." As a matter of fact, on the eve of the Cross, the last night of sleep that Jesus had (when He was able to sleep) was in their house.

2. When Lazarus was seriously ill at home in Bethany—less than two miles from Jerusalem—his sisters sent a brief but tender message via a messenger, "Lord, he whom you love is ill" (3, RSV). No request, but what an elegant appeal! At least the sisters knew Jesus' whereabouts sufficiently to locate Him. When Jesus got the news He said, "This illness is not unto death; it is for the glory of God, so that the Son of God may be glorified by means of it" (4, RSV). Then Jesus made no further mention of the message for two days, then suggested suddenly that they go into Judea again. Immediately His disciples objected with, "Rabbi . . . it is not long since the Jews were wanting to stone you. Are you going there again?" (8, NEB).

Jesus' answer was that there were 12 hours of daylight in a day and pointed out that if He would walk in the daytime He would not stumble in darkness. (The hours were shorter in the wintertime, longer in the summer.) Jesus may be suggesting that duty and devotion combined to make a clear path for Him. He was not about to turn from those sisters who needed and trusted Him. Then He added, "Our friend Lazarus has fallen asleep, but I shall go and wake him" (11, NEB). This gave the disciples some encouragement and they thought that surely Lazarus would recover. But John explains that Jesus had been actually speaking of death as something like sleep. Then Jesus spoke plainly, "Lazarus is dead. I am glad not to have been there; it will be for your good and for the good of your faith. But let us go to him" (14-15, NEB). That settled it. Thomas, the Twin, however blurted out in despair, "Let us also go, that we may die with him" (16, NEB).

3. It was probably an uneasy journey toward Bethany and took about a day. On reaching the outskirts of the village

Jesus found Martha waiting for Him, for the news had reached the older sister that Jesus was on His way.

It must have been a soul-searching time for those two sisters also as they had waited in sorrow. They knew approximately where Jesus was and that it had taken Him three days to get there after their message had reached Him. They recognized some undue delay. So Martha greeted Him, "Lord, if you had been here, my brother would not have died. And even now I know that whatever you ask from God, God will give you" (21-22, RSV). Jesus said to her briefly, "Your brother will rise again" (23, RSV). Martha confessed her faith in the general resurrection at the last day. Jesus spoke particularly now: "I am the resurrection and I am life. If a man has faith in me, even though he die, he shall come to life; and no one who is alive and has faith shall ever die. Do you believe this?" (25-26, NEB). Martha answered, "Lord, I do. I now believe that you are the Messiah, the Son of God who was to come into the world" (27, NEB).

From their conversation (above), it looks like Martha is still thinking of the coming general resurrection, while Jesus is trying to tell her that eternal life is begun even now in terms of a new order of life, and that this order also changes our view of death even now. (See John 17:3.)

4. Presently, Martha ran back for Mary and Jesus stayed on the outskirts of the village until Mary arrived—and it could be that this was prearranged with Jesus. Martha told her sister quietly, "The Master is here; he is asking for you" (28, NEB). Quickly Mary moved to Jesus' location and many of the mourners followed her, supposing she would go to Lazarus' grave to mourn. As soon as Mary came near Jesus she fell at His feet and greeted Him in practically the same words as her sister had. She was in tears and also the women who had followed her were weeping. Jesus "sighed heavily and was deeply moved" (33, NEB).

Then Jesus inquired where they had laid Lazarus and

they replied, "Come and see." Then the record reads simply, "Jesus wept." Here it is rather clear that neither of these devoted women or those surrounding Jesus (including the disciples) were looking for or expecting a resurrection.

5. As they journeyed to the tomb a number were asking themselves and each other, "Could not this man, who opened blind eyes, have done something to keep Lazarus from dying?" (37, NEB). As they approached the tomb, Jesus again sighed deeply. It was a burial in a cave with a large stone placed against the mouth of it. Then Jesus said, "Take away the stone."

At this moment practical Martha objected strenuously. She reminded them that Lazarus had been dead now for four days, and that decay with its offenses would have begun. Jesus replied carefully, "'Did I not tell you that if you have faith you will see the glory of God?' So they removed the stone" (40-41a, NEB).

Some scholars have interpreted the expressions of distress and emotional strain by Jesus as anger, in part. But this does not seem to check with His tears or tenderness. He was moved deeply and the heavy sighs may have been occasioned somewhat by the general unbelief or failure to respond to His challenge to believe. Calvin reminds us that "Christ does not approach the sepulcher as an idle spectator, but as a champion who prepares for a contest; and therefore we need not wonder that he *again* groans; for the violent tyranny of death, which he had to conquer, is placed before his eyes."[14] Calvin also interprets Martha's vehement objection to the removing of the stone at the tomb as the mark of despair. He writes, "While we stretch out the one hand to ask assistance from God, we repel with the other hand that very assistance, as soon as it is offered."[15]

6. Then followed Jesus' prayer. It depicts His tone and outlook better than we can describe or summarize. He looked upwards and prayed: "Father, I thank thee; thou

hast heard me. I knew already that thou always hearest me, but I spoke for the sake of the people standing round, that they might believe that thou didst send me." Following this, Jesus lifted His voice with a great cry: "Lazarus, come forth." The answer follows: "The dead man came out, his hands and feet swathed in linen bands, his face wrapped in a cloth. Jesus said, 'Loose him; let him go'" (43b-44, NEB). Phillips paraphrases, "Let him go home."

In Jesus' request to have the stone removed at the tomb, and in His command to loose Lazarus and let him go, there is an involvement with others as though He would say, "There is no trickery or deception here. It is the power of God alone." Also, when Jairus' daughter was restored to life, Jesus told them to give her something to eat. But He also charged them not to let others know about the restoration. Lazarus makes the third recorded restoration of life by Jesus, but He seems to have exercised a certain restraint at this level of miracle.

7. But Lazarus is not the hope for our resurrection, for he would die again. It was Jesus' own death and resurrection that should afford us the foundation of hope for all mankind. He alone became "the firstfruits of the harvest of the dead" (1 Cor. 15:20b, NEB). Again, "As in Adam all men die, so in Christ all will be brought to life" (1 Cor. 15:22, NEB).

8. The immediate reaction to Lazarus' resurrection is a sad commentary on those who sought to kill the Son of Man. However, some of the visiting Jews from Jerusalem "believed in him." This really means, according to John, that they put their trust in Him, and their trust was genuine. Others went to the Pharisees and reported what had happened.

Then followed a council meeting of what we should call "The Unholy Alliance"—including the ruling priests (Sadducees) and Pharisees. They were totally astonished and frightened, but they covered their selfishness and self-centeredness with pious words and a cloak of concern for their nation. Actually, they did fear a popular uprising and a possible political upheaval, for apparently they had not discovered that Jesus himself had rejected this route as Satan's substitute for the Cross. This council agreed: "If we let him [Jesus] go on thus, every one will believe in him, and the Romans will come and destroy both our holy place and our nation" (48, RSV). Then followed a famous speech by Caiaphas, the current High Priest, which John seems to interpret as an unwitting prophecy concerning the death of Jesus—not only for His own nation, "but to gather together the scattered children of God" (52, NEB). Caiaphas' tone is tinged with arrogance and conceit, and an Americanism would call it "gobbledygook." He said, "You know nothing whatever; you do not use your judgment; it is more to your interest that one man should die for the people, than that the whole nation should be destroyed" (49b-50, NEB).

The die is now cast. "So from that day on they took counsel how to put him to death" (53, RSV). This was not the Sanhedrin meeting; it was an inner, selected group that controlled the Sanhedrin that met unofficially.

Jesus Withdraws to Ephraim
John 11:54-57

> 54   Jesus therefore walked no more openly among the Jews; but went thence unto a country near to the wilderness, into a city called Ephraim, and there continued with his disciples.
> 55   And the Jews' passover was nigh at hand: and many went out of the country up to Jerusalem before the passover, to purify themselves.
> 56   Then sought they for Jesus, and spake among themselves, as they stood in the temple, What think ye, that he will not come to the feast?
> 57   Now both the chief priests and the Pharisees had given a commandment, that, if any man knew where he were, he should shew it, that they might take him.

The withdrawal to Ephraim at this juncture is a combination of Jesus' sense of timing and His recurring need for renewal, especially as the last days came upon Him. The city or town was on the edge of a wilderness region and evidently suited for a hideout. Only His disciples (apostles) were with Him. The news was abroad that Jesus was a "wanted" man, and the Sanhedrin by now had let this be known. The exact location of Ephraim is not known today. It has been estimated to be at a distance of approximately 15 miles from Jerusalem. The length of this withdrawal period is not known; some have guessed it as long as 40 days.

No doubt Jesus was also concentrating on His apostles as they approached the crisis days along with Him. Jesus knew the trauma that awaited them, although they often seemed to want to ignore His immediate warnings.

During this period the Jews were gathering in Jerusalem in preparation for the Passover. There were numerous ceremonial cleansings required that could take a week's time. Besides, it was a crowded affair that would cause many to go early.

Jesus was a frequent topic of conversation among the people. Where is He? Will He come to the feast? And the usual inference was, "Surely He will *not* come?"

But His hour was now coming closer.

The Shadows Lengthen

John 12:1-50

JOHN 12

The Supper and Anointing at Bethany

John 12:1-11

> 1 Then Jesus six days before the passover came to Bethany, where Lazarus was which had been dead, whom he raised from the dead.
> 2 There they made him a supper; and Martha served: but Lazarus was one of them that sat at the table with him.
> 3 Then took Mary a pound of ointment of spikenard, very costly, and anointed the feet of Jesus, and wiped his feet with her hair: and the house was filled with the odour of the ointment.
> 4 Then saith one of his disciples, Judas Iscariot, Simon's son, which should betray him,
> 5 Why was not this ointment sold for three hundred pence, and given to the poor?
> 6 This he said, not that he cared for the poor; but because he was a thief, and had the bag, and bare what was put therein.
> 7 Then said Jesus, Let her alone: against the day of my burying hath she kept this.
> 8 For the poor always ye have with you; but me ye have not always.
> 9 Much people of the Jews therefore knew that he was there: and they came not for Jesus' sake only, but that they might see Lazarus also whom he had raised from the dead.
> 10 But the chief priests consulted that they might put Lazarus also to death;
> 11 Because that by reason of him many of the Jews went away, and believed on Jesus.

Just six days before the Passover, Jesus went to Bethany for a social gathering, and for a dinner given in His honor. What a reunion that must have been, to be with the Bethany trio, again complete! Sure enough, Lazarus was at Jesus' table. Martha was the hostess, as usual.

This could have been the same dinner that was held in the house of Simon the leper and recorded by Matthew and Mark. How fitting that Jesus should consent to go at this time when He was weighed down with the inevitable Cross and the impending crisis for His entire inner circle.

1. Here we have the beautiful scene of "The Extravagance of Love" in which Mary, the sister of Lazarus, poured out a pound (12 ounces in our measure) of very costly perfume, oil of pure nard, and anointed the feet of Jesus (the guest of honor) with it. Then she wiped the ointment off with her own long tresses of hair, until the whole house was filled with the delicate fragrance of it.

Immediately Judas Iscariot burst out with, "Why was this ointment not sold for three hundred denarii [$75.00] and given to the poor? Promptly Jesus came to the rescue, for He saw that Mary's extravagance was the extravagance of love, and He knew that this was a good investment. He replied, "Let her alone, let her keep it for the day of my burial. The poor you always have with you, but you do not always have me" (7-8, RSV).

Morgan comments eloquently: "The radiant loveliness of Mary's action shines like a rainbow of God over the dark clouds that were gathering about Him. In the words of Judas, hell flashed itself out in deep and dire animosity."[1] We are not sure whether Mary had used only a part of the perfume, or perchance Jesus was accepting her total gift now as an advance anointing of His body, in anticipation of His near death.

2. John, the apostle, bristles a bit as he records this scene. He points out that Judas did not really care for the poor, he was the treasurer of their common fund and had been pilfering some out of it. John also reminds us now that it was Judas Iscariot who was to betray Jesus.

No wonder Judas' sense of values was distorted. He planned to betray love; how could he understand the extravagance of love? Waste must be measured in terms of values involved.

3. While they were in Bethany at this time, a great number of Jews came not only to see Jesus, but they came to see the man Lazarus, whom Jesus had raised from the dead. This popularity backfired, for when the chief priests heard of this rising popularity, they planned to kill Lazarus also. What a situation: raised from the dead by the Son of Man and then added to the Most Wanted list by the stone throwers! So far as we know, they never killed Lazarus, but neither he nor his sisters are identified at the scenes of the Cross later on.

(See appendix for a sermon outline on John 12:3*b*.)

The Messianic Triumphal Entry

John 12:12-19

> 12 On the next day much people that were come to the feast, when they heard that Jesus was coming to Jerusalem,
> 13 Took branches of palm trees, and went forth to meet him, and cried, Hosanna: Blessed is the King of Israel that cometh in the name of the Lord.
> 14 And Jesus, when he had found a young ass, sat thereon; as it is written,
> 15 Fear not, daughter of Sion; behold, they King cometh, sitting on an ass's colt.
> 16 These things understood not his disciples at the first: but when Jesus was glorified, then remembered they that these things were written of him, and that they had done these things unto him.
> 17 The people therefore that was with him when he called Lazarus out of his grave, and raised him from the dead, bare record.
> 18 For this cause the people also met him, for that they heard that he had done this miracle.
> 19 The Pharisees therefore said among themselves, Perceive ye how ye prevail nothing? behold, the world is gone after him.

The dinner at Simon's house took place on the evening of the seventh day, for the Sabbath was actually over after sunset. The next day involved the Jewish first day, a week before the Passover.

When the people who had already arrived in Jerusalem for the feast heard that Jesus was coming to Jerusalem, they took palm branches and went out to meet Him.

As they went they shouted, "Hosannah! Blessed is he who comes in the name of the Lord, even the King of Israel!" (13b, RSV). Strictly speaking, the "Hosannahs" were not exclamations of praise; rather, they meant, "Save now!" or "Save, I pray."

1. All of the Gospel writers include this story, and John does not relate some details that others include. The three Synoptists tell us that Jesus sent two of His disciples ahead to find a colt tied and to bring him. Some scholars have assumed that Peter and John might have been sent on this errand, but if so, John does not betray this secret in his account. He simply reports, "Jesus found a young ass and sat upon it" (14, RSV). Two of the writers indicate the young colt had never been ridden before. (Now we know that Jesus was a good equestrian!) This scene in general had been prophesied, John reports: "Fear not, daughter of Zion; behold, your king is coming, sitting on an ass's colt" (15, RSV). Even the disciples did not understand this at the time, but after that Jesus was glorified it came into clear perspective for them.

2. Palms were emblems of victory and were used at the Feast of Tabernacles, and probably at certain other religious exercises or festivals. John, the Revelator, tells of a vast throng he saw, "from every nation . . . and languages, standing in front of the throne and before the Lamb. They were robed in white and had palms in their hands, and they shouted together: "Victory to our God who sits on the throne, and to the Lamb!" (7:9-10, NEB).

The crowd that was going to welcome Jesus were those who had witnessed the power of God through Jesus in the resurrection of Lazarus. The prophecy concerning the lowliness of their coming King came from Zechariah:

> "Rejoice greatly, O daughter of Zion!
> Shout aloud, O daughter of Jerusalem!
> Lo, your king comes to you;
> triumphant and victorious is he,

humble and riding on an ass,
on a colt the foal of an ass.
I will cut off the chariot from Ephraim
and the war horse from Jerusalem;
and the battle bow shall be cut off,
and he shall command peace to the nations;
his dominion shall be from sea to sea,
and from the River to the ends of the earth"
(Zech. 9:9-10, RSV).

Here is the Messiah divinely promised—so contrary to the surges of their nation's cries—but in harmony with the Father's will and mission and the economy of Redemption to be so dearly purchased.

The Greeks Inquire for Jesus; Jesus Again Withdraws

John 12:20-43

20 And there were certain Greeks among them that came up to worship at the feast:
21 The same came therefore to Philip, which was of Bethsaida of Galilee, and desired him, saying, Sir, we would see Jesus.
22 Philip cometh and telleth Andrew: and again Andrew and Philip tell Jesus.
23 And Jesus answered them, saying, The hour is come, that the Son of man should be glorified.
24 Verily, verily, I say unto you, Except a corn of wheat fall into the ground and die, it abideth alone: but if it die, it bringeth forth much fruit.
25 He that loveth his life shall lose it; and he that hateth his life in this world shall keep it unto life eternal.
26 If any man serve me, let him follow me; and where I am, there shall also my servant be: if any man serve me, him will my Father honour.
27 Now is my soul troubled; and what shall I say? Father, save me from this hour: but for this cause came I unto this hour.
28 Father, glorify thy name. Then came there a voice from heaven, saying, I have both glorified it, and will glorify it again.
29 The people therefore, that stood by, and heard it, said that it thundered: others said, An angel spake to him.
30 Jesus answered and said, This voice came not because of me, but for your sakes.
31 Now is the judgment of this world: now shall the prince of this world be cast out.
32 And I, if I be lifted up from the earth, will draw all men unto me.
33 This he said, signifying what death he should die.
34 The people answered him, We have heard out of the law that Christ abideth forever: and how sayest thou, The Son of man must be lifted up? who is this Son of man?

In this lesson John records the final incident of the public ministry of Jesus contained in the four Gospels. It very likely followed the day of questions and answers that Matthew records so carefully. This discourse occurred two days before the Passover. Following this public display, Jesus retired to Bethany for the quiet of that friendly scene there.

1. The Greeks came through Philip to find audience with Jesus. These were either "God-fearers" or Gentile proselytes who had been circumcised. At least they were there to worship at the feast, in the Gentile court. Their plea was an eloquent one, "Sir, we would see Jesus." Philip checked with Andrew and together they went to Jesus.

Jesus' reply seems to relate more to the disciples and the total audience than to the Greeks, except by inference. Jesus himself appears to be preoccupied with the crisis then upon Him, and it was climactic—so He answered with a fitting sense of destiny that only He could employ: "The hour is come for the Son of man to be glorified" (23, RSV).

2. This phrase "to be glorified" is used by John in three instances; here, at the Last Supper when Judas had finally

left them to betray his Lord, and in the high priestly prayer in intimacy with the Father (John 17:1). Some have wondered how Jesus knew so clearly that His hour was come. We can only suggest that His sense of destiny and mission remained crystal clear by His own uncontested obedience to the Father's will. Even in the hour of heartbreak and turmoil, He turned away from the natural cry to be saved from that hour. His own answer John records clearly: "Now is my soul troubled. And what shall I say? Father, save me from this hour? No, for this purpose I have come to this hour. Father, glorify thy name" (27, RSV). Here we like Phillips' translation of Heb. 1:3 in which Jesus is identified with the Father as, "This Son, radiance of the glory of God, faultless expression of the nature of God."

3. In the heart of Jesus' reply He lays down the principle of life through death. He finds it illustrated in the grain of seed that must die in order to produce a harvest. Jesus insists, "He that loveth his life shall lose it; and he that hateth his life in this world shall keep it unto life eternal" (25). Temple puts it clearly and concisely: "Self-love is self-destruction; self-centredness is sin, and self-love is hell."[2]

Jesus would demonstrate this principle to the full in His own life by the Cross, and afford us redemption. But He also lays down the same principles for those who would follow Him. Their chief reward He promised was God himself and a climate that would be eternally endurable and radiant.

4. But in telling of the Cross before Him, Jesus really answered the Greeks. His death was to be for all. The "whosoever" of John 3:16-17 and the love demonstrated and expounded on the Cross could not be confined to a chosen people. These were really called to explain that the elections of God were for inclusion rather than for exclusion, as many had assumed selfishly. So here is the real answer to the Greeks (or Gentile world), "I, if I be lifted up from

the earth, will draw all men unto me" (32). What a final declaration for all mankind, and for every generation! Morris states it clearly, "The gospel is the gospel for the whole world only because of the Cross."[3]

Jesus, the Father's Own Agent

John 12:44-50

> 44 Jesus cried and said, He that believeth on me, believeth not on me, but on him that sent me.
>
> 45 And he that seeth me seeth him that sent me.
>
> 46 I am come a light into the world, that whosoever believeth on me should not abide in darkness.
>
> 47 And if any man hear my words, and believe not, I judge him not: for I came not to judge the world, but to save the world.
>
> 48 He that rejecteth me, and receiveth not my words, hath one that judgeth him: the word that I have spoken, the same shall judge him in the last day.
>
> 49 For I have not spoken of myself; but the Father which sent me, he gave me a commandment, what I should say, and what I should speak.
>
> 50 And I know that his commandment is life everlasting: whatsoever I speak therefore, even as the Father said unto me, so I speak.

The public ministry of Jesus ends with this portion of scripture. In a sense, Jesus is summarizing the heart of His message. The tone as expressed when He "cried aloud" speaks of urgency, significance and climax. Again the appeal is to believe, not for the sake of Jesus, but rather because of the Father who had sent Him, and the authoritative finality of the message He had given to His Son.

There is no railing in this last word, for the sacredness and accuracy of His message came from the Father. In truth, Jesus puts it very strongly when He says, "For I have not spoken on my own authority; the Father who sent me has himself given me the commandment what to say and what to speak" (49, RSV). In other words, "What I say, therefore I say as the Father has bidden me" (50, RSV). This is why Jesus insists that His mission is not essentially one of judgment, but He acknowledges that His word will stand to judge "on the last day." He is careful to insist that His principal assignment is to bring light, but the rejection of His redemptive message in the end means darkness remains upon them.

Morris quotes Barrett's summary here: "Jesus is not a figure of independent greatness; he is the Word of God, or He is nothing at all."[4] The power of this appeal is not that of sheer authority; it rises from the motivation of God himself, redeeming love, as expressed by the Son of God himself.

Final Discourses and Events

John 13:1—17:26

JOHN 13

Upper Room Ministry and Example

John 13:1-20

1 Now before the feast of the passover, when Jesus knew that his hour was come that he should depart out of this world unto the Father, having loved his own which were in the world, he loved them unto the end.

2 And supper being ended, the devil having now put into the heart of Judas Iscariot, Simon's son, to betray him;

3 Jesus knowing that the Father had given all things into his hands, and that he was come from God, and went to God;

4 He riseth from supper, and laid aside his garments; and took a towel and girded himself.

5 After that he poureth water into a bason, and began to wash the disciples' feet, and to wipe them with the towel wherewith he was girded.

6 Then cometh he to Simon Peter: and Peter saith unto him, Lord, dost thou wash my feet?

7 Jesus answered and said unto him, What I do thou knowest not now; but thou shalt know hereafter.

8 Peter saith unto him, Thou shalt never wash my feet. Jesus answered him, If I wash thee not, thou hast no part with me.

9 Simon Peter saith unto him, Lord, not my feet only, but also my hands and my head.

10 Jesus saith to him, He that is washed needeth not save to wash his feet, but is clean every whit: and ye are clean, but not all.

11 For he knew who should betray him; therefore said he, Ye are not all clean.

12 So after he had washed their feet, and had taken his garments, and was set down again, he said unto them, Know ye what I have done to you?

13 Ye call me Master and Lord. and ye say well; for so I am.

14 If I then, your Lord and Master, have washed your feet; ye also ought to wash one another's feet.

15 For I have given you an example, that ye should do as I have done to you.

16 Verily, verily, I say unto you, The servant is not greater than his lord; neither he that is sent greater than he that sent him.
17 If ye know these things, happy are ye if ye do them.
18 I speak not of you all: I know whom I have chosen: but that the scripture may be fulfilled, He that eateth bread with me hath lifted up his heel against me.
19 Now I tell you before it come, that, when it is come to pass, ye may believe that I am he.
20 Verily, verily, I say unto you, He that receiveth whomsoever I send receiveth me; and he that receiveth me receiveth him that sent me.

The next two chapters (13 and 14) relate the story of the Upper Room ministry. The scene changes to another location in the three chapters that follow (15, 16, and 17). But all five chapters shine with divine radiance and glory against the deep darkness of hatred and entrenched wickedness in high places that surround them. These are the farewell discourses and fraught with far-reaching significance. They speak to our hearts today. Jesus himself is the central figure and teacher par excellence. His words have a simplicity and depth that probes us.

1. The calendar was just before the Passover festival. The climactic hour of the Cross is upon Him and Jesus is sensitively aware of it. John in his Gospel points up the master key to the situation in the latter half of verse one: "He had loved his own who were in the world, and now he was to show the extent of his love" (1b, NEB). This is the explanation before it happened. Here the Cross is not simply a tragedy brought on be evil and unjust men. Neither was it the martytdom of a good man, strangely misunderstood. This death afforded a redemption, divinely provided and proffered to all mankind.

John now hints more specifically that meanwhile the devil had entered into the heart of Judas Iscariot, Simon's son, to betray Jesus. But we shall postpone this discussion into the next section of scripture.

2. Then followed the foot washing scene, a lesson the inner group could never forget. Jesus assumed the position of a slave. He divested himself of his outer garments and clothed himself with a large towel and proceeded to wash

His disciples' feet. The order in which He began is not given. Some have supposed He began with Judas or John, but we don't know. When He got to Peter, he protested vehemently. In substance he said, "Not *me,* Lord." Jesus promptly acknowledged that Peter didn't really understand now the true meaning of what He was doing, but at a later date he would. Jesus insisted by saying, "If I do not wash you, you are not in fellowship with me" (8*b*, NEB). Then Peter wanted Jesus to wash his hands and head as well, But Jesus held him to the simple foot washing that was usually done before the meal by a slave; now Jesus performs the act himself during the meal.

3. MacGregor observes keenly, "Peter is humble enough to see the incongruity of Christ's action, yet proud enough to dictate to his Master."[1] All of this is highlighted in the Synoptic account by the immediate dispute among the disciples as to which of them would be the greatest. This background also explains in part why Jesus did it in the midst of the meal. It could have been a spontaneous and unplanned setting for that lesson. No wonder Jesus made the application immediately: "Then if I, your Lord and Master, have washed your feet, you also ought to wash one another's feet. I have set you an example: you are to do as I have done for you" (14-15, NEB). In some respects this beautiful scene comes as a climactic drama from the self-emptying of the Son of God become man among men.

Richardson sees this incident as pointing to the Cross itself. He writes, "It foreshadows the cross itself; the voluntary humility of the Lord cleanses his loved ones and gives to them an example of selfless service which they must follow."[2]

Jesus closes this lesson by enumerating the chain of command (climbing upward) in the message and mission of redemption. It is as clear as one, two, three. "In very truth I tell you, he who receives any messenger of mine receives me; receiving me, he receives the One who sent me" (20, NEB).

The Prophecy of Betrayal

John 13:21-30

21 When Jesus had thus said, he was troubled in spirit, and testified, and said, Verily, verily, I say unto you, that one of you shall betray me.
22 Then the disciples looked one on another, doubting of whom he spake.
23 Now there was leaning on Jesus' bosom one of his disciples, whom Jesus loved.
24 Simon Peter therefore beckoned to him, that he should ask who it should be of whom he spake.
25 He then lying on Jesus' breast saith unto him, Lord, who is it?
26 Jesus answered, He it is, to whom I shall give a sop, when I have dipped it. And when he had dipped the sop, he gave it to Judas Iscariot, the son of Simon.
27 And after the sop Satan entered into him. Then said Jesus unto him, That thou doest, do quickly.
28 Now no man at the table knew for what intent he spake this unto him.
29 For some of them though, because Judas had the bag, that Jesus had said unto him, Buy those things that we have need of against the feast; or, that he should give something to the poor.
30 He then having received the sop went immediately out: and it was night.

This is a sad story, that a man chosen to be a disciple and apostle of Jesus Christ should finally betray his Lord to His enemies. It was actually a betrayal of love; only an insider could do that.

In the account of Mary of Bethany's act of love in anointing Jesus with that costly ointment (John 12:3-6), John is careful to point out that Judas Iscariot's real interest in that occasion was not the poor, but himself. As we noted earlier, Judas was the treasurer of the common fund, and apparently had already been pilfering some for himself in carrying on his duties. John hints that this was part of Judas' moral breakdown.

1. *Judas Iscariot was chosen as the others,* after prayer by Jesus and with the avowed intent of making him a pillar in the Master's kingdom venture. Many have tried to probe Judas' mind after the fact in order to discover the real inner clash. It does look now that he was disappointed in Jesus when He failed to accept the acclaim given him

by the populace and their effort to make Him a king. Judas was interested in an earthly kingdom eventually.

2. *Jesus was faithful to warn and guide Judas*—even as He did the others. When some of the disciples (followers) had turned back on Jesus because of His spiritual accents, He said to the 12, "Will you also go away?" (John 6:67, RSV). Peter responded with a strong declaration and loyalty. Then Jesus followed up with the strong warning: "Did I not choose you, the twelve, and one of you is a devil?" (6:70, RSV). John explains carefully in his record, "He spoke of Judas, the son of Simon Iscariot, for he, one of the twelve, was to betray him" (6:71, RSV).

3. *Jesus also appealed to Judas with the intimacy of friendship and with a responsible assignment expressing confidence in him.* He recognized his gifts and made him treasurer of their common fund. At that last meal together, he probably sat on the right of Jesus, with John on the left. We are sure that Jesus washed Judas' feet, too, as He did the rest, despite His knowledge of a bribe pledge already received against his Master.

4. *Jesus never gave up on Judas, even when Judas had apparently gone over to the other side for personal gain.* It was then that "Jesus exclaimed in deep agitation of spirit, 'In truth, in very truth, I tell you, one of you is going to betray me'" (21, NEB). Even then Judas had agreed on a bribe and the proposition was his own. The Jewish leaders bargained with him in the amount, thirty pieces of silver, the price of a slave.

5. *Judas woke up when it was too late.* After Jesus was condemned to die, Judas returned the bribe money to the chief priests and elders, and cried with great remorse, "I have sinned; I have brought an innocent man to his death" (Matt. 27:4a, NEB). But those men wouldn't accept the return of their money and said, "What is that to us? See to that yourself" (Matt. 27:4b, NEB).

It was a black night when Judas forsook that company of apostles after their last meal together, but now it was the blackest day of all when he threw down the 30 pieces of silver in the temple and went out and hanged himself (Matt. 27:5).

A line from Francis Thompson's great lyric poem *The Hound of Heaven* fits this sad ending, "All things betray thee, who betrayest me."

A New Commandment of Love

John 13:31-35

> 31 Therefore, when he was gone out, Jesus said, Now is the Son of man glorified, and God is glorified in him.
>
> 32 If God be glorified in him, God shall also glorify him in himself, and shall straightway glorify him.
>
> 33 Little children, yet a little while I am with you. Ye shall seek me: and as I said unto the Jews, Whither I go, ye cannot come; so now I say to you.
>
> 34 A new commandment I give unto you, That ye love one another; as I have loved you, that ye also love one another.
>
> 35 By this shall all men know that ye are my disciples, if ye have love one to another.

The instruction by Jesus in the Upper Room is begun with love. In some respects it is not a new commandment, except that is a new order or measure of love—His own love for His disciples. In fact, His love furnishes us the motive and the power needed.

Here is the last time that Jesus identifies himself with His favorite name, Son of man. But His emphasis is upon the Cross. It reveals the nature and heart of God, the Father.

Jesus reveals that love must be the identifying mark of His disciples. It is the universal mark for all people, in all times and places. Tertullian quoted long ago the comment of the heathen about Christians in general: "See, they say, how they love one another." Even today in heathen lands, as well as at home, people most quickly learn what we believe by our lives.

The tenderness of Jesus seems more acute as He runs out of time. He has a feeling for their dilemma just before them. Here He calls them, "Little children." This is no thundering command as He soon will leave them. It is like a deathbed wish and prayer, for only the abiding issues that now loom up before Him are worthy of His time and attention.

The Prophecy of Peter's Denial

John 13:36-38

> 36 Simon Peter said unto him, Lord, whither goest thou? Jesus answered him, Whither I go, thou canst not follow me now; but thou shalt follow me afterwards.
>
> 37 Peter said unto him, Lord, why cannot I follow thee now? I will lay down my life for thy sake.
>
> 38 Jesus answered him, Wilt thou lay down thy life for my sake? Verily, verily, I say unto thee, The cock shall not crow, till thou hast denied me thrice.

The quick summary of Jesus' prophecy concerning Peter's denial of his Lord is told in all the Gospel accounts, but it is John who is careful to reveal an inside story of Peter's restoration in John 21:15-19. In all of the Synoptic accounts of this scene now before us, Jesus warns all of His 11 disciples that they will fall away or lose their faith in Him. He quotes the scripture prophecy in confirmation, "I will smite the shepherd, and the sheep shall be scattered."

Peter argued with his Lord and insisted that he would go all the way with Him—even to death itself. Then Jesus said, "Will you indeed lay down your life for me? I tell you in very truth, before the cock crows you will have denied me three times" (38).

Peter is silent then for a while until they came to arrest Jesus and Peter spoke with his sword. But Jesus rebuked him and said, "Sheathe your sword. This is the cup my Father has given me; shall I not drink it?" (John 18: 17, NEB).

Strength and Guidance Promised
Through the Holy Spirit

John 14:1-31

1 Let not your heart be troubled: ye believe in God, believe also in me.

2 In my Father's house are many mansions: if it were not so, I would have told you. I go to prepare a place for you.

3 And if I go and prepare a place for you, I will come again, and receive you unto myself; that where I am, there ye may be also.

4 And whither I go ye know, and the way ye know.

5 Thomas saith unto him, Lord, we know not whither thou goest; and how can we know the way?

6 Jesus saith unto him, I am the way, the truth, and the life: no man cometh unto the Father, but by me.

7 If ye had known me, ye should have known my Father also: and from henceforth ye know him, and have seen him.

8 Philip saith unto him, Lord, shew us the Father, and it sufficeth us.

9 Jesus saith unto him, Have I been so long time with you, and yet hast thou not known me, Philip? he that hath seen me hath seen the Father; and how sayest thou then, Shew us the Father?

10 Believest thou not that I am in the Father, and the Father in me? the words that I speak unto you I speak not of myself: but the Father that dwelleth in me, he doeth the works.

11 Believe me that I am in the Father, and the Father in me: or else believe me for the very works' sake.

12 Verily, verily, I say unto you, He that believeth on me, the works that I do shall he do also; and greater works than these shall he do; because I go unto my Father.

13 And whatsoever ye shall ask in my name, that will I do, that the Father may be glorified in the Son.

14 If ye shall ask any thing in my name, I will do it.

15 If ye love me, keep my commandments.

16 And I will pray the Father, and he shall give you another Comforter, that he may abide with you for ever;

17 Even the Spirit of truth; whom the world cannot receive, because it seeth him not, neither knoweth him: but ye know him; for he dwelleth with you, and shall be in you.

18 I will not leave you comfortless: I will come to you.

19 Yet a little while, and the world seeth me no more; but ye see me: because I live, ye shall live also.

20 At that day ye shall know that I am in my Father, and ye in me, and I in you.

21 He that hath my commandments, and keepeth them, he it is that loveth me: and he that loveth me shall be loved of my Father, and I will love him, and will manifest myself to him.

22 Judas saith unto him, not Iscariot, Lord, how is it that thou wilt manifest thyself unto us, and not unto the world?

23 Jesus answered and said unto him, If a man love me, he will keep

my words: and my Father will love him, and we will come unto him, and make our abode with him.

24 He that loveth me not keepeth not my sayings: and the word which ye hear is not mine, but the Father's which sent me.

25 These things have I spoken unto you, being yet present with you.

26 But the Comforter, which is the Holy Ghost, whom the Father will send in my name, he shall teach you all things, and bring all things to your remembrance, whatsoever I have said unto you.

27 Peace I leave with you, my peace I give unto you: not as the world giveth, give I unto you. Let not your heart be troubled, neither let it be afraid.

28 Ye have heard how I said unto you, I go away, and come again unto you. If ye loved me, ye would rejoice, because I said, I go unto the Father: for my Father is greater than I.

29 And now I have told you before it come to pass, that, when it is come to pass, ye might believe.

30 Hereafter I will not talk much with you: for the prince of this world cometh, and hath nothing in me.

31 But that the world may know that I love the Father; and as the Father gave me commandment, even so I do. Arise, let us go hence."

1. *Talking to Troubled Disciples*

This sacred discourse is addressed to our Lord's inner circle, but the truth and applications contained belong to all believers and to all who would follow Jesus.

Jesus is talking to troubled men—they had been shaken greatly by the content of their Master's recent words (c. 13). They had left all to follow Him; now after some three and a half years, He is about to leave them. He told them frankly that they could not follow Him.

Also, with deep agitation of spirit, He had told them with certainty that one of them would betray Him. Only one of the inner band who were inquiring knew for sure who the guilty party was, for the man was their trusted treasurer, a man of some gifts and apparent leadership. Added to this came the shattering word that Peter, their ready leader and frequent spokesman would deny his Lord three times at a certain hour very soon.

a. All these warnings were intended to prepare them a bit. But now Jesus moves into the real issue, their faith in God and their trust in himself. We rather like the paraphrase or rewording of verse one on the NEB: "Set your troubled hearts at rest. Trust in God always; trust also in me."

Jesus also reassures them of the ultimate outcome. The house of God as their destiny is sure. Even the silence of God in issues that now trouble them are not on the side of uncertainty or doubt or lack of planning. What an eloquent tribute to God, "If it were not so I should have told you" (2, NEB). There is a permanent reunion ahead. They will eventually be at home in the house of God, even as He.

b. The real answer to their abiding, biting questions lies in Jesus himself. He spells it out again to all through puzzled Thomas' bewilderment and inquiry: "I am the way; I am the truth; and I am the life; no one comes to the Father except by me" (6, NEB). We are not sure, but it reads like Thomas was asking for a theophany (a visible appearance of God), like Moses had in the wilderness pasture that was his. But Jesus' reply was, "If you knew me you would know my Father too. From now on you do know him; you have seen him" (7, NEB).

Barclay comments here: "It may well be that to the ancient world this was the most ataggering thing that Jesus ever said. To the Greeks God was characteristically *The Invisible.* The Jew could count it as an article of faith that no man has seen God at any time."[3]

c. Jesus now identifies himself and His work with the Father and challenges them to judge Him by His works. But He also astounds them further by concluding, "In truth, in very truth I tell you, he who has faith in me will do what I am doing; and he will do greater things still because I am going to the Father. Indeed anything you ask in my name I will do, so that the Father may be glorified in the Son. If you ask anything in my name I will do it" (12-14, NEB). "In my name" here is not a magic wand or an Open Sesame of fairyland style, it is an ethical condition of obedience and moral likeness. It is the extension of redemption through His disciples, noted well at the ingathering on the day of Pentecost and in subsequent missionary evangelism among the Gentiles begun at first by Paul and Barnabas.

(1) But look at Jesus the Way—they killed Him, for He was truly dead when they went to break His legs with the mallet or hammer.

(2) He is also the Truth, but lies prevailed and Judaism contrived and outwitted the Roman governor until they crucified the Son of man (Roman style).

(3) He is also the Life, and yet His body became a corpse and was properly buried as such.

d. But God's abiding answer is a resurrection. His own Son became the "firstfruits of the harvest of the dead" (1 Cor. 15:20b, NEB). This would be a good time to sing one of our favorite hymns in the form of a resolution, born of the Spirit of God:

I am resolved no longer to linger,
Charmed by the world's delight;
Things that are higher, things that are nobler,
These have allured my sight.

I am resolved to go to the Saviour,
Leaving my sin and strife.
He is the true One; He is the just One;
He hath the words of life.

I am resolved to follow the Saviour,
Faithful and true each day,
Heed what He sayeth, do what He willeth;
He is the living Way.

I am resolved to enter the Kingdom,
Leaving the paths of sin.
Friends may oppose me, foes may beset me;
Still will I enter in.

Refrain:
I will hasten to Him,
Hasten so glad and free.
Jesus, Greatest, Highest,
I will come to Thee.

—Palmer Hartsough

Jesus not only prepares the house of God for us; He also prepares us for that house so we will be at home in the will and presence of God.

(See appendix for a sermon outline on John 14:1-2.)

2. *The Promise of the Comforter*

In facing up to the shattering experience that was to confront His inner circle on His death, Jesus presents the next step in the economy of grace, the gift of the Holy Spirit. To be sure, He had spoken of Him earlier in John 7:37-39, and John had given us the clear exegesis of that passage in his record. With perspective he warned even then that the Spirit would be given after Jesus was glorified. Now the day is drawing nearer, so Jesus pulls back the curtain some more on the divine mission and strategy of redemption. Jesus assures that inner group that He will not leave them bereft or without a leader or guide. He will ask the Father and He will send them another to be their Advocate or Counselor or Strengthener. But there is a moral and ethical demand upon those who receive Him. The world is excluded—they "cannot receive [him], because it neither sees him nor knows him; you know him, for he dwells with you, and will be in you" (17, RSV). Jesus spells it out: "If you love me you will obey my commands; and I will ask the Father, and he will give you another to be your Advocate, who will be with you for ever—the Spirit of truth" (15-16, NEB).

a. Two later references to the Holy Spirit complete Jesus' revelation of Him at the time.

(1) "When the Counselor comes, whom I will send to you from the Father, even the Spirit of truth, who proceeds from the Father, he will bear witness to me; and you also are witnesses, because you have been with me from the beginning" (15:26-27, RSV).

(2) "When the Spirit of truth comes, he will guide you into all the truth; for he will not speak on his own authority, but whatever he hears he will

speak, and he will declare to you the things that are to come. He will glorify me, for he will take what is mine and declare it to you. All that the Father has is mine; therefore I said that he will take what is mine and declare it to you" (16:13-15, RSV).

In commenting on the first passage above, John Wesley observes in his *Notes upon the New Testament:* "The Spirit's coming, and being sent by our Lord from the Father, to testify of Him, are personal characters, and plainly distinguish Him from the Father and the Son; and His title as *the Spirit of truth,* together with His proceeding from the Father, can agree to none but a divine person. And that He proceeds from the Son, as well as from the Father, may be fairly argued from His being called 'The Spirit of Christ' (1 Pet. 1:11), and from His being here said to be sent by Christ from the Father, as well as sent by the Father in His name."[4]

b. Here, too, we should observe that to identify the Holy Spirit constantly and simply as the Spirit of Jesus tends to ignore His person and deny the trinity of the Godhead. To be sure, He will exalt Jesus, but He also manifests the Father. The Holy Spirit comes by mission from the Father, even as the Son came by the Father.

The Holy Spirit has often been identified as the Comforter and was thus used by Wyclif in his translation. Temple reminds us, however, that "Wyclif certainly understood it as meaning 'strengthener' (comforter) rather than 'consoler'; the suggestion is of one who makes us brave and strong by being brave and strong beside us. But to strengthen is the best of all ways to console, for it brings a bracing consolation and not a relaxing sympathy."[5]

Lightfoot underscores that the Holy Spirit's work as the Spirit of Truth is not an operation independent of the life and teaching of Jesus. To be sure, "He both knows (and indeed is) all truth and also imparts truth to believers." Lightfoot explains: "It thus becomes clear that, just as the Lord has full knowledge of the Father, so the Spirit has full knowledge of the Son, and will impart this knowledge to believers, as they are able to receive it. But the work of the Spirit will and must consist solely in 'bringing to remembrance' the Lord's teaching; the Lord being one with the Father, and the disciples being admitted to the presence of the Father only in and through the Son, no advance beyond the Lord in His historical manifestation is or ever will be possible."[6]

c. In the foregoing, Jesus has been preparing His inner circle for the cataclysm of the Cross as it would fall on these whom He had chosen to carry on His mission. But He is also trying to teach them that the divine plan does include a new Advocate or Strengther for them. He shows that in the end it will be better for them also. His mission was temporary, for a little while; whereas the new Counselor will abide with them forever.

In these last hours together Jesus underscores the significance of practical obedience. "The man who has received my commands and obeys them—he it is who loves me; and he who loves me will be loved by my Father; and I will love him and disclose myself to him" (21, NEB). Here Jesus puts love and obedience in perspective and relationship. Morgan shows the interaction and balance here: "Obedience is the demonstration of love. Love, therefore, is the inspiration of obedience."[7] Jesus would almost say, "They are Siamese twins." There is a sense in which love is never lawless nor careless about God's delights. Paul wrote in the Roman letter, "Note then the kindness and the severity of God: severity toward those who have fallen, but God's kindness to you, provided you continue in his kindness; otherwise you too will be cut off" (11:22, RSV). This is no idle threat; this is the reality of wholesome Christian living. Carelessness when constant is the antithesis of devotion and love.

But the mood of inner victory prevails with Jesus throughout. He acknowledges that the clash with the powers of evil is imminent. He confesses, "The ruler of this world is coming. He has no power over me; but I do as the Father has commanded me, so that the world may know that I love the Father" (30b-31, RSV).

"Rise, let us go hence" is the courageous close (31b).

Holy Ghost, with light divine,
Shine upon this heart of mine.
Chase the shades of night away;
Turn my darkness into day.

Holy Ghost, with power divine,
Cleanse this guilty heart of mine.
Long hath sin without control
Held dominion o'er my soul.

Holy Ghost, with joy divine,
Cheer this saddened heart of mine.
Bid my many woes depart;
Heal my wounded, bleeding heart.

Holy Spirit, all divine,
Dwell within this heart of mine.
Cast down ev'ry idol throne;
Reign supreme, and reign alone.

—ANDREW REED

John 15

Jesus the True Vine

John 15:1-27

1 I am the true vine, and my Father is the husbandman.
2 Every branch in me that beareth not fruit he taketh away: and every branch that beareth fruit, he purgeth it, that it may bring forth more fruit.
3 Now ye are clean through the word which I have spoken unto you.
4 Abide in me, and I in you. As the branch cannot bear fruit of itself, except it abide in the vine; no more can ye, except ye abide in me.
5 I am the vine, ye are the branches: He that abideth in me, and I in

him, the same bringeth forth much fruit: for without me ye can do nothing.

6 If a man abide not in me, he is cast forth as a branch, and is withered; and men gather them, and cast them into the fire, and they are burned.

7 If ye abide in me, and my words abide in you, ye shall ask what ye will, and it shall be done unto you.

8 Herein is my Father glorified, that ye bear much fruit; so shall ye be my disciples.

9 As the Father hath loved me, so have I loved you: continue ye in my love.

10 If ye keep my commandments, ye shall abide in my love; even as I have kept my Father's commandments, and abide in his love.

11 These things have I spoken unto you, that my joy might remain in you, and that your joy might be full.

12 This is my commandment, That ye love one another, as I have loved you.

13 Greater love hath no man than this, that a man lay down his life for his friends.

14 Ye are my friends, if ye do whatsoever I command you.

15 Henceforth I call you not servants; for the servant knoweth not what his lord doeth: but I have called you friends; for all things that I have heard of my Father I have made known unto you.

16 Ye have not chosen me, but I have chosen you, and ordained you, that ye should go and bring forth fruit, and that your fruit should remain: that whatsoever ye shall ask of the Father in my name, he may give it you.

17 These things I command you, that ye love one another.

18 If the world hate you, ye know that it hated me before it hated you.

19 If ye were of the world, the world would love his own: but because ye are not of the world, but I have chosen you out of the world, therefore the world hateth you.

20 Remember the word that I said unto you, The servant is not greater than his lord. If they have persecuted me, they will also persecute you; if they have kept my saying, they will keep yours also.

21 But all these things will they do unto you for my name's sake, because they know not him that sent me.

22 If I had not come and spoken unto them, they had not had sin: but now they have no cloak for their sin.

23 He that hateth me hateth my Father also.

24 If I had not done among them the works which none other man did, they had not had sin: but now have they both seen and hated both me and my Father.

25 But this cometh to pass, that the word might be fulfilled that is written in their law, They hated me without a cause.

26 But when the Comforter is come, whom I will send unto you from the Father, even the Spirit of truth, which proceedeth from the Father, he shall testify of me:

27 And ye also shall bear witness, because ye have been with me from the beginning.

At the close of the previous chapter Jesus and His apostles left the Upper Room with the apparent intention of facing the inevitable crisis of the Cross. It looked like

Jesus might head for Gethsemane immediately, but we have no record from John concerning the beleaguered band crossing over the brook Kidron to their favorite garden spot until the opening lines of the 18th chapter. It could have been that Jesus was staying out of sight until He had completed the most intimate discourses recorded in the next chapters.

1. Jesus now opens with, "I am the true [real] vine, and my Father is the husbandman [gardener] (1). The background for this in the Old Testament is the fact that Israel was formerly known as God's own vine. Psalm 80 sings in part:

"Thou didst bring a vine out of Egypt;
thou didst drive out nations and plant it;
thou didst clear the ground before it,
so that it made good roots and filled the land" (8-9, NEB).

But something happened, for now.

"The wild boar from the thickets gnaws it,
and swarming insects from the fields feed on it" (13, NEB).

The refrain appears and closes the appeal,

"Lord God of Hosts, restore us;
make thy face shine upon us that we may be saved" (19, NEB).

The same idea that a vine gone to pieces symbolizes a nation that has departed from God appears in several of the prophets. Jeremiah chapter 12 is typical:

"Many shepherds have ravaged my vineyard and trampled down my field,
They have made my pleasant field a desolate wilderness,
made it a waste land, waste and waterless, to my sorrow.
The whole land is waste, and no one cares. (10-11, NEB).

Now in John 15 Jesus changes the figure: He himself

is the true vine (real), tended by our Heavenly Father. The relatively small group of disciples (especially the inner circle addressed) constitute the branches. The fruit or growth comes from the intimacy and oneness of the vine and the branches. The fruit in this case indicates the expansion of His true kingdom.

The pattern has been set by our Lord himself. At first glance it looks like a great bonanza—a huge, limitless giveaway program. Who could hesitate? But when we examine it carefully we may find, as one hunter put it, "A bear trap with grass on it." But that is not a fair description. It is an "if and then" proposition.

2. The measure or nature of abiding in our Lord has its source and example in the Father and the Son themselves. "As the Father has loved me, so have I loved you; continue ye in my love. If ye keep my commandments, ye shall abide in my love; even as I have kept my Father's commandments, and abide in his love" (9-10). This is the real key to the wide-open invitation, "Ye shall ask what ye will, and it shall be done unto you" (7), but it is preceded by the "if" of the true fellowship and ethical obedience. Morgan writes, "The nature of the union is that of the love-mastered life that demonstrates our loyalty to our Lord, and allows Him to express himself through us in fruit."[8]

3. No mention here is made of skilled techniques or how other successful disciples are doing it. It is a divine franchise afforded us, and the fruit is inevitable if we dare to ask in faith. The Father himself, according to Jesus, is committed to make us fruit bearing—not only much fruit but fruit that remains (5-16). Here the emphasis is a balance between quality and quantity.

But fruit bearing is the Church's business. We cannot dodge it. We are a part of the divine mission, even as Jesus was in affording it when He came as the incarnate Son. The worst phase of failing to abide in the vine is our fruitlessness. Sanguine or smug self-content is sin. To that extent we cancel the divine purpose through us.

4. There is also definite evidence that this fruit bearing constitutes the Father's glory and is, in a measure, the touchstone of true discipleship (8). But there is inevitable pruning that is in the Father's hands. He also will afford the needed cleansing necessary to produce fruitfulness. This cannot be simulated or duplicated on the human level. Man's utter dependence here is painstakingly clear as Jesus states it unequivocally: "Apart from me you can do nothing" (5b, RSV).

Quinby summarizes it well; "Fruitfulness is the public insignia of a believer,"[9] and yet he is seldom self-conscious about it. But it is the fruit-bearing Christian who makes it easier for sinful men and women to believe in God and want to draw near to Him.

5. In these hours when lengthened and foreboding shadows hung all around Him like a threatening storm, Jesus dared to speak (for the first time) of His joy. It seems that He could already feel the lift of victory before the final clash. This must have been what the writer in the Book of Hebrews had detected: "Jesus who, for the sake of the joy that lay ahead of him, endured the cross, making light of its disgrace, and has taken his seat at the right hand of the throne of God" (12:2, NEB).

But Jesus plainly shows the following as a principal motivation for the divine commands He had given them. He concludes, "I have spoken thus to you, so that my joy might be in you, and your joy complete" (11, NEB). But the overall atmosphere of this victorious mood would arise from the experiential fact that these disciples were loving one another and this love was comparable to the love of the Father and the Son.

6. Also, in a last-ditch effort to fortify His noble band for the onslaughts of persecution that would surround them

in a special way after His departure, He warns: "If the world hates you, it hated me first, as you know well. If you belonged to the world, the world would love its own; but because you do not belong to the world, for that reason the world hates you. Remember what I said: 'A servant is not greater than his master.' As they persecuted me, they will persecute you; they will follow your teaching as little as they have followed mine. It is on my account that they will treat you thus, because they do not know the One who sent me" (18-21, NEB).

This summary just quoted reminds us of an Irishman's soliloquy concerning his enemies. He sang: "They scorned us just for being what we are." Jesus puts it stronger than that; He says in substance, "They will hate you because they actually hate me and my Father also" (23). Here is a hint at what Paul wrote about later on to the church at Philippi: "All I care for is to know Christ, to experience the power of his resurrection, and to share his sufferings, in growing conformity with his death, if only I may finally arrive at the resurrection from the dead" (3:10-11, NEB).

Temple observes openly: "The true disciple still offers to the world a challenge, which it will take up if his faithfulness is active. Not all that the world hates is good; but it does hate good Christianity." He also suggests that "the world is the most dangerous of the three great enemies," largely because "against the world we must stand alone with our fellow Christians."[10]

But Jesus is saying, "Persecution is inevitable; expect it!" Ryle points out with some penetration, "It is not the weakness and inconsistencies of Christians that the world hates, but their grace."[11] The defense of the Christian in the day of persecution is God himself. Martin Luther's hymn reminds us that the right Man is on our side, even today.

> *A mighty Fortress is our God,*
> *A Bulwark never failing;*

Our Helper He, amid the flood
   Of mortal ills prevailing.
For still our ancient foe
Doth seek to work us woe;
His craft and power are great,
And, armed with cruel hate,
On earth is not his equal.

Did we in our own strength confide,
   Our striving would be losing,
Were not the right Man on our side,
   The Man of God's own choosing.
Dost ask who that may be?
Christ Jesus, it is He;
Lord Sabbaoth, His name,
From age to age the same,
And He must win the battle.

And though this world, with devils filled,
   Should threaten to undo us,
We will not fear, for God has willed
   His truth to triumph through us.
The prince of darkness grim—
We tremble not for him,
His rage we can endure,
For, Lo! his doom is sure;
One little word shall fell him.

That word above all earthly powers,
   No thanks to them, abideth;
The Spirit and the gifts are ours
   Through Him who with us sideth.
Let goods and kindred go,
This mortal life also;
The body they may kill;
God's truth abideth still.
His kingdom is forever.

The Holy Spirit to Become Permanent Teacher

John 16:1-33

1 These things have I spoken unto you, that ye should not be offended.

2 They shall put you out of the synagogues: yea, the time cometh, that whosoever killeth you will think that he doeth God service.

3 And these things will they do unto you, because they have not known the Father, nor me.

4 But these things have I told you, that when the time shall come, ye may remember that I told you of them. And these things I said not unto you at the beginning, because I was with you.

5 But now I go my way to him that sent me; and none of you asketh me, Whither goest thou?

6 But because I have said these things unto you, sorrow hath filled your heart.

7 Nevertheless I tell you the truth; It is expedient for you that I go away: for if I go not away, the Comforter will not come unto you; but if I depart, I will send him unto you.

8 And when he is come, he will reprove the world of sin, and of righteousness, and of judgment:

9 Of sin, because they believe not on me;

10 Of righteousness, because I go to my Father, and ye see me no more;

11 Of judgment, because the prince of this world is judged.

12 I have yet many things to say unto you, but ye cannot bear them now.

13 Howbeit when he, the Spirit of truth, is come, he will guide you into all truth: for he shall not speak of himself; but whatsoever he shall hear, that shall he speak: and he will shew you things to come.

14 He shall glorify me: for he shall receive of mine, and shall shew it unto you.

15 All things that the Father hath are mine: therefore said I, that he shall take of mine, and shall shew it unto you.

16 A little while, and ye shall not see me: and again, a little while, and ye shall see me, because I go to the Father.

17 Then said some of his disciples among themselves, What is this that he saith unto us, A little while, and ye shall not see me: and again, a little while, and ye shall see me: and, Because I go to the Father?

18 They said therefore, What is this that he saith, A little while? we cannot tell what he saith.

19 Now Jesus knew that they were desirous to ask him, and said unto them, Do ye enquire among yourselves of that I said, A little while, and ye shall not see me: and again, a little while, and ye shall se me?

20 Verily, verily, I say unto you, That ye shall weep and lament, but the world shall rejoice: and ye shall be sorrowful, but your sorrow shall be turned into joy.

21 A woman when she is in travail hath sorrow, because her hour is come: but as soon as she is delivered of the child, she remembereth no more the anguish, for joy that a man is born into the world.

22 And ye now therefore have sorrow: but I will see you again, and your heart shall rejoice, and your joy no man taketh from you.

23 And in that day ye shall ask me nothing. Verily, verily, I say unto you, Whatsoever ye shall ask the Father in my name, he will give it you.

24 Hitherto have ye asked nothing in my name: ask, and ye shall receive, that your joy may be full.

25 These things have I spoken unto you in proverbs: but the time cometh, when I shall no more speak unto you in proverbs, but I shall shew you plainly of the Father.

26 At that day ye shall ask in my name: and I say not unto you, that I will pray the Father for you:

27 For the Father himself loveth you, because ye have loved me, and have believed that I came out from God.

28 I came forth from the Father, and am come into the world: again, I leave the world, and go to the Father.

29 His disciples said unto him, Lo, now speakest thou plainly, and speakest no proverb.

30 Now are we sure that thou knowest all things, and needest not that any man should ask thee: by this we believe that thou camest forth from God.

31 Jesus answered them, Do ye now believe?

32 Behold, the hour cometh, yea, is now come, that ye shall be scattered, every man to his own, and shall leave me alone: and yet I am not alone, because the Father is with me.

33 These things I have spoken unto you, that in me ye might have peace. In the world ye shall have tribulation: but be of good cheer; I have overcome the world.

1. *Persecution Foretold* (1-4)

This chapter is actually a continuation of chapter 15. We get the feeling that Jesus is very much aware that He is running out of time. Areas of concern that He could not talk about in advance, He must crowd in now enough to warn and prepare His apostles for the immediate future. Again, Jesus is the Master Teacher. He could not tell them everything at once; it would floor them.

Now He warns them of persecution, not simply from an evil world of sin, but from a religious people, His own Judaism. In fact, persecution will become part of their religion. He warned, "They will ban you from the synagogue, indeed, the time is coming when anyone who kills you will suppose he is performing a religious duty" (2, NEB). But Jesus insisted that the real reason for this situation was "because they do not know either the Father or me" (3, NEB). Jesus explained that His chief reason for telling them now was to guard against the breakdown of their faith.

Saul of Tarsus confessed, after he became the missionary apostle Paul, that he was guilty of all this because he was "ardent in God's service" as were the leading Jews of his day. In writing to the Corinthian church Paul confessed, "For I am the least of the apostles, unfit to be called an apostle, because I persecuted the Church of God" (1 Cor. 15:9, RSV). Paul testified also that grace had saved him: "But by the grace of God I am what I am, and his grace toward me was not in vain" (1 Cor. 15:10, RSV). Morris observes: "It is the tragedy of religious man that he so often regards persecution as in line with the will of God."

2. *The Work of the Holy Spirit in Redemption* (5-15)

a. Actually, Jesus had not begun to prepare His apostles for His death upon the Cross until the last six months of His ministry. Now He assures them that another Teacher or Advocate will carry on in His stead. There were things that He wanted to tell them that they could not stand now; they would be overloaded with grief and perplexities. Here Jesus indicates a parallelism between the Holy Spirit and himself like unto the relationship between Jesus and the Father. He says, "He [the Spirit of truth] will glorify me, for everything that he makes known to you he will draw from what is mine. All that the Father has is mine, and that is why I said, 'Everything that he makes known to you he will draw from mine'" (14-15, NEB). So ultimately the source of truth is the Father himself.

b. The work of the Holy Spirit (as Counselor or Advocate) Jesus insisted was to their advantage. He was not to come on a limited term basis as Jesus had operated, but He was to abide. Also, His work was to be built on the atoning death of Christ, Jesus' resurrection, and His ascension to the Father. Jesus said plainly, "If I go not away, the Counselor (or Advocate) will not come to you;

but if I go, I will send Him to you. And when He comes, He will convince the world of sin and of righteousness and of judgment" (see 7b-8).

Morgan observes that "with the awakening of the spiritual side of a man's nature there ever comes to him a threefold consciousness: a consciousness of sin, a consciousness of righteousness, a consciousness of judgment." All of this, he insists, "is after all but one, the consciousness of God."[13] But this is essentially the redemptive mission of the unseen but real Holy Spirit. In Jesus' explanation He identifies sin with unbelief in himself; He relates righteousness to His return to the Father with 'mission accomplished'; He looks at judgment in an ultimate sense, showing that the prince of this world stands condemned and defeated.

c. The Holy Spirit reveals sin in its essence as against God and His moral order. The prodigal who returned home acknowledged the basis of his own defeat and despair because he had "sinned against heaven" and before his father. But Jesus, the Savior, accepted the responsibility and consequences of our sins as a human race and made them His own. John the Baptist had introduced Jesus as "the Lamb of God; it is he who takes away the sin of the world" (John 1:29, NEB). Later on, Paul wrote to Titus concerning our Savior Christ Jesus: "He it is who sacrificed himself for us, to set us free from all wickedness, and to make us a pure people marked out for his own, eager to do good" (2:14, NEB).

d. But sin is also unbelief and, by inference at least, a rejection of His atoning death. Jesus affords us the righteous way by His atoning death. He was more than the sinless One. On His return to the Father He became the exalted One at the right hand of God the Father. Morgan reminds us: "He came there not merely as the perfect Man. He came there wounded, with scars in His hands, and feet, and side."[14] But His message shines out, "I am he that liveth." Purity and Holiness had triumphed! Barrett sees the death and resurrection of Jesus as showing the righteousness of Christ and of God: "Jesus' death proved his complete obedience to the will of God, and his exaltation proved that his righteousness was approved by more than human acclamation."[15]

e. There is also the final judgment and defeat of sin. By His own victory, Jesus announced in advance "by showing that the Prince of this world stands condemned" (11, NEB). No wonder He could say without hesitation, "But I shall see you again, and then you will be joyful, and no one shall rob you of that joy" (22b, NEB).

f. In more recent years some have made the Paraclete essentially a Spirit of Praise or a Spirit of Ecstasy, but His deepest mission is that of Spirit of Truth. Morris points out clearly and soundly: "The work of the Spirit is Christocentric. He will draw attention not to Himself but to Christ. He will glorify Christ. It is the things of Christ that He takes and declares, i.e., His ministry is built upon and is the necessary sequel to that of Christ." However, Morris also reminds us carefully, "There is no division in the Godhead."[16] The economy of grace gives a place of executive leadership to the Holy Spirit, but He honors the Father and the Son—and never himself.

3. *The Disciples' Perplexity Answered* (16-24)

a. In an effort to acknowledge that they had now almost run out of time, Jesus uses the clause "A little while, and you will see me no more" (16a, RSV). Then He adds another clause, "again a little while, and you will see me" (16b). It all adds up to confusion or contradiction. They talked to each other about this double conundrum and the added explanation, "Because I go to the Father" (17b, RSV). This didn't help them either. They couldn't figure out what He meant by "a little while" used in this puzzling situation.

Jesus sensed that they wanted to talk about this, so He brought it up. His explanation was, "Truly, truly, I say to you, you will weep and lament, but the world will rejoice; you will be sorrowful, but your sorrow will turn into joy" (20, RSV). Then He illustrated the mother's travail and sorrow in childbirth, but on the advent of the child joy takes over, and she no longer remembers her former anguish. Jesus seems to imply, "That will be your situation, too." Then He adds, "So you have sorrow now, but I will see you again and your hearts will rejoice, and no one will take your joy from you" (22, RSV).

It then seems fairly clear that Jesus was reading their hearts' sorrow at His approaching death, and He was trying to reassure them that He would return and then they would be truly glad. He insisted that their latter joy would be abiding, enduring. Jesus' anticipated victory thus appears as a silver lining. But we have no clear evidence that the disciples really took it in except in the Master's word. John writes, of course, with an after-the-fact perspective, but he tells the story as it really happened and recreates the mood and outlook that prevailed at that time.

b. Then Jesus offered them the new day when they could accept prayer—as the Father intended it—in Jesus' absence, but in His name. He concludes, "In that day you will ask nothing of me. Truly, truly, I say to you, if you ask anything of the Father, he will give it to you in my name. Hitherto you have asked nothing in my name; ask, and you will receive that your joy may be full" (23-24, RSV).

Morris observes, "It may be significant that He does not speak of their sorrow being replaced by joy, but of turning into it. The very same thing, the Cross, that would be to them first a cause of sorrow would later become a source of joy."[17] Calvin also adds a thought, "Christ means that the sorrow which they will endure for the sake of the Gospel will be fruitful."[18]

It is rather apparent now that Jesus was talking about His death on the Cross that would throw His apostles and disciples into a "blue funk," but all of this would change after His return in resurrection. The new mind and mood then obtained would be permanent and triumphant. There is no doubt about it now, that the Resurrection was a necessary precursor to Pentecost and the divine enabling that would follow.

4. *The Disciples' Faith Declared and Peace Assured* (25-33)

Throughout the past three chapters Jesus has referred to "the Father" more than 40 times. Now He assures them that the Father himself loves them (His apostles or inner circle) because they have loved Jesus and believed that He came from the Father. Then He spells it out simply: "I came from the Father and have come into the world; again, I am leaving the world and going to the Father" (28, RSV). His disciples replied, "Ah, now you are speaking plainly, not in any figure! Now we know that you know all things, and need none to question you; by this we believe that you come from God" (29-30, RSV). But Jesus still questions them and warns them, "Do you now believe? The hour is coming, indeed it has come, when you will be scattered, every man to his own home, and will leave me alone; yet I am not alone, for the Father is with me" (31-32, RSV). Then as though to undergird them in that fearful hour added: "I have said this to you, that in me you may have peace. In the world you have tribulation; but be of good cheer, I have overcome the world" (33, RSV).

Lightfoot observes, "Although the world is the object of God's love (3:16), it remains to the end and must remain, a battlefield. In this battlefield, however, victory already lies with the Lord, and is therefore guaranteed also to His followers."[19] Here Jesus speaks with high courage and inner confidence. He has overcome, therefore He could offer them the final word of peace, not as a formal good-by, but as a genuine benediction. Morris observes fittingly here, "The church depends ultimately on what God has done in Christ, not on the courage and wit of its first members."[20] Dodd also points out carefully, "It is part of the character and genius of the Church that its foundation members were discredited men; it owed its existence not to their faith, courage or virtue, but to what

Christ had done with them; and this they could never forget."[21]

Here is an old hymn that we learned in Scotland; it is much older than our memory:

Peace, perfect peace, in this dark world of sin?
The blood of Jesus whispers peace within.

Peace, perfect peace, by thronging duties pressed?
To do the will of Jesus—this is rest.

Peace, perfect peace, our future all unknown?
Jesus we know; and He is on the throne.

It is enough; earth's struggles soon shall cease!
And Jesus calls us to heaven's perfect peace.

JOHN 17

The High Priestly Prayer

John 17:1-26

1 These words spake Jesus, and lifted up his eyes to heaven, and said, Father, the hour is come; glorify thy Son, that thy Son also may glorify thee:
2 As thou hast given him power over all flesh, that he should give eternal life to as many as thou hast given him.
3 And this is life eternal, that they might know thee the only true God, and Jesus Christ, whom thou hast sent.
4 I have glorified thee on the earth: I have finished the work which thou gavest me to do.
5 And now, O Father, glorify thou me with thine own self with the glory which I had with thee before the world was.
6 I have manifested thy name unto the men which thou gavest me out of the world: thine they were, and thou gavest them me; and they have kept thy word.
7 Now they have known that all things whatsoever thou hast given me are of thee.
8 For I have given unto them the words which thou gavest me; and they have received them, and have known surely that I came out from thee, and they have believed that thou didst send me.
9 I pray for them: I pray not for the world, but for them which thou hast given me; for they are thine.

10 And all mine are thine, and thine are mine; and I am glorified in them.

11 And now I am no more in the world, but these are in the world, and I come to thee. Holy Father, keep through thine own name those whom thou hast given me, that they may be one, as we are.

12 While I was with them in the world, I kept them in thy name: those that thou gavest me I have kept, and none of them is lost, but the son of perdition; that the scripture might be fulfilled.

13 And now come I to thee; and these things I speak in the world, that they might have my joy fulfilled in themselves.

14 I have given them thy word; and the world hath hated them, because they are not of the world, even as I am not of the world.

15 I pray not that thou shouldest take them out of the world, but that thou shouldest keep them from the evil.

16 They are not of the world, even as I am not of the world.

17 Sanctify them through thy truth: thy word is truth.

18 As thou hast sent me into the world, even so have I also sent them into the world.

19 And for their sakes I sanctify myself, that they also might be sanctified through the truth.

20 Neither pray I for these alone, but for them also which shall believe on me through their word;

21 That they all may be one; as thou, Father, art in me, and I in thee, that they also may be one in us: that the world may believe that thou hast sent me.

22 And the glory which thou gavest me I have given them; that they may be one, even as we are one:

23 I in them, and thou in me, that they may be made perfect in one; and that the world may know that thou hast sent me, and hast loved them, as thou hast loved me.

24 Father, I will that they also, whom thou hast given me, be with me where I am; that they may behold my glory, which thou hast given me: for thou lovedst me before the foundation of the world.

25 O righteous Father, the world hath not known thee: but I have known thee, and these have known that thou hast sent me.

26 And I have declared unto them thy name, and will declare it: that the love wherewith thou hast loved me may be in them, and I in them.

If prayer reveals the inner and true nature of our religious life, then this seventeenth chapter of John is a mountain peak and serves as the "holy of holies" in the divine disclosure of the Son of God, made manifest as the Son of Man. Temple observes, "There is no cause for wonder that in this prayer, offered as His ministry approaches its climax and close, the Lord should make this a central theme—*that thou didst send Me.*"[22] The curtains are drawn back here on the intimacy between the Father and the Son. John the Apostle again staggers us a bit with the combined profundity and simplicity that mingle in these penetrating lines. But the eloquence is essentially that of truth rather than of euphony. It is the longest recorded prayer of Jesus in the Gospels.

It was a sacred hour for Jesus and the chosen 11 who were with Him. He had finished His assignment—except for the Cross before Him—and He was thoroughly committed to that. The next step in the divine strategy involved especially the 11 who would carry on. The Master knew full well the cataclysmic effect of the Cross on these whom He had chosen. They were badly shaken already by His own recent disclosures to them, and He sensed their needed reinforcement. But Jesus was not gloomy or despairing, for His most recent word to them was: "I have told you all this so that in me you may find peace. In the world you will have trouble. But courage! The victory is mine: I have conquered the world" (16:33, NEB).

Milligan and Moulton in their commentary on John caution us: "No attempt to describe the prayer can give a just idea of its sublimity, its pathos, its touching yet exalted character, its tone at once of tenderness and triumphant expectation."[23] Some have observed that the prayer itself is an expansion of the Lord's prayer in content, tone, and approach. Jesus begins with, "Father, the hour is come; glorify thy Son that the Son may glorify thee" (1*b*, RSV). Here the obedience of the Son is mingled with the majesty of the Father. But even as He prayed "he lifted up his eyes to heaven" (1). At the very outset we get the feeling that we are on "holy ground" as we listen in.

The Cross before Him is both the occasion and cause for this prayer, and its chief burden is the 11 disciples who are the key to Jesus' entire ministry and the instruments of its extension. This special hour (the Cross) has hovered over the Master throughout His entire ministry, and more especially during the last six months. In this period Jesus had been carefully preparing His inner group for the final hour now upon them. But His own approaching death and the sharp separation now upon them was not a day of doom or gloom to Jesus, the Son; it was an occasion to bring glory to both the Father and the Son, in that order.

1. *Jesus Prays for Himself* (1-5)

a. This beginning prayer is no soliloquy or a session in self-contemplation; it is a personal sharing with the Father and a mission-accomplished report. Jesus prays for the Father's manifest presence in the hours ahead: "Now, Father, glorify me in thy own presence with the glory which I had with thee before the world was made" (5, RSV). Jesus had just acknowledged the power over all mankind that the Father had given Him (2). But this power was not given for self-glorifying on Jesus' part, except as the Father might be glorified through His challenge ahead and the victories of the Cross. Temple summarizes the heart of this part of Jesus' petition, "The Cross is the focus of eternal glory." He reasons, "In one sense it is true to say that the death on the Cross was the gateway to that eternal fellowship and glory, but more profoundly it is true to say that the death on the Cross is itself the attainment of that fellowship and glory in absolute plenitude."[24]

The message of Hebrews is rather pertinent here: "Although he was a Son, he learned obedience through what he suffered: and being made perfect he became the source of eternal salvation to all who obey him, being designated by God a high priest after the order of Melchizedek" (5: 8-10, RSV).

b. Thirteen times throughout this entire prayer Jesus indicates the Father's gifts to Him, and some four references are made of the Son's gifts to the disciples. Abbot explains, "What *grace* is in the Pauline epistles, *giving* is in the Fourth Gospel." However, we do recall the emphasis of the Prologue as John gave it: "For the law was given by Moses, but grace and truth came by Jesus Christ" (1:16).

c. In the early part of the prayer Jesus identifies himself as the sent one and names himself as Jesus Christ. This compound noun is found in John's Gospel only here in verse 3 and in 1:16. He thus identifies himself as the promised Messiah, although He had amended the current

Jewish political concept of Messiah. To Jesus, their basic need was spiritual deliverance.

Jesus identifies eternal life, born of a relationship and personal knowledge with the Father and the Son (3). It is far more than unending life; it is a new order of life.

2. *Jesus Prays for His Disciples* (6-19)

a. Here Jesus is careful to report with thanksgiving that He had already told His disciples—given to Him by the Father—conceiving the source of His own teaching; it was the Father himself. He reports a rewarding reception on their part: "They have kept thy word" (6*b*). He epitomizes: "Now they know that everything that thou has given me is from thee; for I have given them the words which thou gavest me, and they have received them and know in truth that I came from thee; and they have believed that thou didst send me" (7-8, RSV). Thus Jesus accounts for His stewardship now entrusted to the inner circle.

b. But Jesus' real burden is for these 11 apostles who will carry on when He goes. Also, He is looking to the immediate cataclysm that would fall on them at His death. He reminded the Father that the economy of grace would be entrusted to their care: "As thou didst send me into the world, so I have sent them into the world" (18, RSV). Their safety and steadfastness are now all important. Hear Him pray: "And now I am no more in the world, but they are in the world, and I am coming to thee. Holy Father, keep them in thy name, which thou hast given me that they may be one, even as we are one" (11, RSV). Jesus further reports, "While I was with them, I kept them in thy name, which thou hast given me; I have guarded them, and none of them is lost but the son of perdition, that the scripture might be fulfilled" (12, RSV).

We have already discussed in summary the betrayal of Judas (John 13:21-30), but here we should observe that the relation between Judas' deed and the divine prophecy are sometimes confused. One careful scholar actually identifies Judas as the devil incarnate! But this seems to us a gratuitous assumption to equate the power of the Adversary to be equal with God. It also makes prophecy involving foretelling causative and eventually puts the blame on God for men's evil deeds. Then what does it do to Jesus' perception in the prayerful choice of His disciples who became apostles? (See John 2:25).

c. In His prayer Jesus reminds the Father that His chosen group had made the break with the world. He declares plainly, "They are not of the world, even as I am not of the world" (16). But more than all Jesus prays that they may be delivered "from the evil one." Hear Him: "I do not pray that thou shouldst take them out of the world, but that thou shouldst keep them from the evil one" (15, RSV).

d. The heart of Jesus' prayer for His disciples on the positive side is when He prays, "Sancfity them through thy truth: thy word is truth: (17). Just prior to this He had reminded the Father, "They are not of the world, even as I am not of the world" (16).

All of this relates to the redemptive mission (mentioned above) to which Jesus had assigned them (18). This identical assignment is repeated in a post-resurrection appearance on that memorable first day of the week when He appeared unexpectedly with the greeting, "Peace be with you" (20:21, RSV).

This was more than a consecration to their holy task; it was to prepare their hearts inwardly for their task. To be sure Jesus also said, "And for their sakes I sanctify myself, that they also might be sanctified through the truth" (19, RSV). Phillips' translation helps in understanding here. In verse 17, he translates: "Make them holy by the truth; for your word is the truth." Verse 19, he translates, "I consecrated myself for their sakes that they may be made holy by the truth."

Here it is evident that the Word of God, including the

total gospel of grace, is the instrumental cause for our sanctification, both for life and service. But the meritorious cause is the Cross, we turn to Hebrews again: "And so Jesus also suffered outside the city gate to make his people holy through his own blood" (13:12, NIV).

Luthi, commenting on "I sanctify myself," writes carefully, "The One who says it now is the first and last to do so. . . . It is the Son who is able to say the exceptional words, 'I sanctify myself'. . . . This absolute, voluntary, filial obedience is the secret of Christ's self-sanctification." Then Luthi explores verse 19 also: "'For their sakes.' That is the all-important thing here; 'I sanctify myself for their sakes.' Their holiness is not self-acquired; it is given to them, and what gift it is!"[25]

Hoskyns also lays the groundwork for our sanctification in the atoning death of our Lord. He writes: "The Lord had thus, in the presence of His disciples, consecrated Himself to death as the effective sacrifice upon which their sanctification was to depend, and He had solemnly dedicated them to the mission which was to be the effective result of His death and resurrection."[26] Hoskyns concludes that the efficacy of Jesus' teaching was grounded in the efficacy of His sacrificial death. Thus Hoskyns sees "No separation between Word and Work."[27]

(See appendix for a sermon outline on John 17:17.)

3. *Jesus Prays for All Who Will Believe* (20-26)

As we read the Gospel of John, there is no way to separate the love of God and the gift of His Son (John 3: 16-17). But the love of God extends to His disciples, and before this high priestly prayer closes, it reaches beyond them. "I do not pray only for these men but for all those who will believe in me through their message" (20, Phillips). The same applies to Christ's prayer for the sanctification of future believers. Luthi expands his insight at this point also: "Christ's sanctification of Himself does not stop short at the disciples. Because He dies for the eleven and sanctifies Himself 'for their sakes', far more than these eleven men are affected. By sanctifying Himself for their sakes, He sanctifies Himself for every person who will let the disciples call him into the Kingdom of the Son."[28]

The prayer that began with the 11 apostles had reached round the world.

Jesus closes His prayer with confidence in the Father. What a beautiful salutation, "Righteous Father"; beautiful combination! Phillips has paraphrased it, "Father of goodness and truth."

Let the prayer of Jesus sing in our hearts today.

> *Majestic sweetness sits enthroned*
> *Upon the Saviour's brow;*
> *His head with radiant glories crowned,*
> *His lips with grace o'erflow.*
>
> *No mortal can with Him compare*
> *Among the sons of men;*
> *Fairer is He than all the fair*
> *Who fill the heavenly train.*
>
> *He saw me plunged in deep distress,*
> *And flew to my relief;*
> *For me He bore the shameful cross,*
> *And carried all my grief.*
>
> *Since from His bounty I receive*
> *Such proofs of love divine,*
> *Had I a thousand hearts to give,*
> *Lord, they should all be thine.*
>
> —SAMUEL STENNETT

Jesus' Arrest, Trial, and Execution

John 18:1—19:42

JOHN 18

Jesus Surrenders in the Garden

John 18:1-11

> 1 When Jesus had spoken these words, he went forth with his disciples over the brook Cedron, where was a garden, into the which he entered, and his disciples.
> 2 And Judas also, which betrayed him, knew the place: for Jesus ofttimes resorted thither with his disciples.
> 3 Judas then, having received a band of men and officers from the chief priests and Pharisees, cometh thither with lanterns and torches and weapons.
> 4 Jesus therefore, knowing all things that should come upon him, went forth, and said unto them, Whom seek ye?
> 5 They answered him, Jesus of Nazareth. Jesus saith unto them, I am he. And Judas also, which betrayed him, stood with them.
> 6 As soon then as he had said unto them, I am he, they went backward, and fell to the ground.
> 7 Then asked he them again, Whom seek ye? And they said, Jesus of Nazareth.
> 8 Jesus answered, I have told you that I am he: if therefore ye seek me, let these go their way:
> 9 That the saying might be fulfilled, which he spake, Of them which thou gavest me have I lost none.
> 10 Then Simon Peter having a sword drew it, and smote the high priest's servant, and cut off his right ear. The servant's name was Malchus.
> 11 Then said Jesus unto Peter, Put up thy sword into the sheath: the cup which my Father hath given me, shall I not drink it?

Throughout the Gospel of John the word and work of Jesus intertwine. Much of the time the work came first and the teaching or meaning followed. In the immediate chapters preceding this one, the teaching came first, and it seems that Jesus was using His instruction now to prepare the inner circle for the crisis upon Him. But the crisis itself was not forced upon Jesus; He came by the Father's appointment and the Cross makes up the heart of His mission. Its efficacy also looms before them.

1. Jesus' mood—while weighed down by the delicacy of the situation involving these men who had left all to follow Him—is one of triumph. He goes out to meet those who had come to arrest Him. But He states His own terms for surrender—"If you seek me, let these men go" (8, RSV). Also, the arresting group "drew back and fell to the ground" when Jesus actually identified himself. This was no ordinary peasant they had come to arrest! There was a majestic dignity to this Jewish teacher.

It is interesting that it was in a garden where the encounter with the arresting group took place, led by Judas. He knew this familiar spot where Jesus and His disciples had frequently gone previously for seclusion. An "insider" was the traitor. Some scholars also assume that Jesus and His disciples had often slept here in the open air, possibly in a tent.

2. The arresting group was made up of some Temple guards, plus a knot of Roman soldiers. (A similar Temple guard had failed to arrest Jesus previously when sent on a similar errand by the Jews, 7:44 ff.). The arresting group came equipped with lanterns, torches, and weapons as they found Jesus in His favorite prayer garden. They twice named their desired man as "Jesus of Nazareth," and twice He said, "I am he."

3. At this juncture, "Simon Peter, who had a sword, drew it and slashed at the High Priest's servant, cutting off his right ear" (10, Phillips). The servant (or slave) was named Malchus. "Then said Jesus unto Peter, Put up thy sword into the sheath: the cup which my Father hath given me, shall I not drink it?" (11). Calvin comments: "It was exceedingly thoughtless in Peter to try to prove his faith by his sword, while he could not do so by his tongue. When

he is called to make a confession, he denies, but now un-
bidden by His Master he raises a tumult."[1]

It was Luke who recorded that when the group came
to arrest Jesus and Judas had betrayed Him with a kiss,
as soon as His followers had perceived fully what was taking place they asked, "Lord, shall we strike with the
sword?" (22:49, RSV). It was then that Peter slashed out
at the high priest's slave. "But Jesus said, 'No more of
this!' And he touched his ear and healed him" (22:51,
RSV). Commenting on this, Redding writes: "The unbe-
lievable miracle is that Jesus had the presence of mind to
look for that missing ear in the grass at Gethsemane, and
that He had the thoughtfulness to put it back where it
belonged. . . . Who cares about someone's ear at a time
that makes all the difference in the world? Jesus cared,
and on His way to the Cross He stooped down to pick up
someone's ear and put it back."[2]

"So the band of soldiers and their captain and the
officers of the Jews seized Jesus and bound him" (12,
RSV).

Trial Before Annas (Ecclesiastical)

John 18:12-14, 19-24

> 12 Then the band and the captain and officers of the Jews took Jesus,
> and bound him,
> 13 And led him away to Annas first; for he was father in law to
> Caiaphas, which was the high priest that same year.
> 14 Now Caiaphas was he, which gave counsel to the Jews, that it was
> expedient that one man should die for the people.
>
> 19 The high priest then asked Jesus of his disciples, and of his doc-
> trine.
> 20 Jesus answered him, I spake openly to the world; I ever taught in
> the synagogue, and in the temple, whither the Jews always resort; and
> in secret have I said nothing.
> 21 Why askest thou me? ask them which heard me, what I have said
> unto them: behold, they know what I said.
> 22 And when he had thus spoken, one of the officers which stood by
> struck Jesus with the palm of his hand, saying, Answerest thou the high
> priest so?
> 23 Jesus answered him, If I have spoken evil, bear witness of the evil:
> but if well, why smitest thou me?
> 24 Now Annas had sent him bound unto Caiaphas the high priest.

None of the other Gospel writers mentions that Jesus came before Annas, the former high priest. John does record the fact that he was father-in-law to Caiaphas, the current high priest. In the strictest sense of Jewish law, Annas was the legitimate high priest. This examination could have been a preliminary affair and might have been either a "fishing expedition" for self-incriminating evidence, or it could have been a courtesy assignment out of respect to Annas' standing among the Jews themselves. Annas had been deposed by the Roman governor, the predecessor of Pilate. He was succeeded in his office by his five sons and the current high priest, Caiaphas, was his son-in-law. He was also known as Joseph.

In actual fact, the priestly aristocracy was better known for its intrigue and bribery rather than for its jurisprudence or piety.

In John's account Jesus came before Annas first (13), and then was sent to Caiaphas (24). In looking at the time situation, it looks as though Annas' hearing was at night and Caiaphas' audience was in the early morning. The latter could have taken place in the same general area.

It is difficult to believe that the entire Sanhedrin was present at this preliminary hearing when a police officer of the Temple slapped Jesus openly in the face without protest. Jesus answered him without timidity, "If I spoke amiss, state it in evidence; if I spoke well, why strike me?" (23, NEB). The presiding high priest had "questioned Jesus about his disciples and about what he taught" (19, NEB). Jesus' reply to the presiding judge was: "I have spoken openly to all the world; I have always taught in the synagogue and in the temple, where all Jews congregate; I have said nothing in secret. Why question me? Ask my hearers what I told them; they know what I said" (20-21, NEB).

The dilemma brought on by the face-slapping incident evidently broke up the hearing. "So Annas sent him bound to Caiaphas the High Priest" (24, NEB).

Some have wondered why Jesus didn't turn the other

cheek to the court officer. Actually, Jesus was reminding the judge that no evidence had been heard and the San-hedrin's legal procedure was that a man is considered absolutely innocent and cannot be cross-examined until the evidence was in. Also, Augustine answered those who quote Matthew 5:39 here with, "Those great precepts of His are to be fulfilled not by bodily ostentation, but by the preparation of the heart. For it is possible that even an angry man may visibly hold out his other cheek. How much better, then, is it for one who is inwardly pacified to make a truthful answer, and with tranquil mind hold himself ready for the endurance of heavier sufferings to come."[3]

Peter's Denial

John 18:15-18, 25-27

> 15 And Simon Peter followed Jesus, and so did another disciple; that disciple was known unto the high priest, and went in with Jesus into the palace of the high priest.
> 16 But Peter stood at the door without. Then went out that other disciple, which was known unto the high priest, and spake unto her that kept the door, and brought in Peter.
> 17 Then saith the damsel that kept the door unto Peter, Art not thou also one of this man's disciples? He saith, I am not.
> 18 And the servants and officers stood there, who had made a fire of coals; for it was cold: and they warmed themselves: and Peter stood with them, and warmed himself.
>
> 25 And Simon Peter stood and warmed himself. They said therefore unto him, Art not thou also one of his disciples? He denied it, and said, I am not.
> 26 One of the servants of the high priest, being his kinsman whose ear Peter cut off, saith, Did not I see thee in the garden with him?
> 27 Peter then denied again: and immediately the cock crew.

In his account of Peter's denial, John separates the first denial from the second and third. In fact, there could be a brief interval of time between all three denials. John does not always tell his stories in strict sequence of time, but it would not be necessary to assume there was a great gap of time between any of the tests that confronted Peter.

1. Jesus had warned Peter that he would deny Him, but He had also warned that "the hour is coming, indeed it

has come, when you will be scattered, every man to his home, and will leave me alone" (John 16:32, RSV). Both of these were fulfilled soon after Jesus' arrest. Matthew records it, "Then all the disciples forsook him, and fled" (26:56).

But Peter and John recovered enough to follow the scene of action presently. John in this case identifies himself as "another disciple" (15). It was he who gained entrance to the court of the high priest for both of them.

2. Peter's test first came from the maid that kept the door. She said, "Are not you also one of this man's disciples?" He said, "I am not" (17, RSV). Peter had committed himself in denial and it would be difficult to reverse himself. Chyrsostom defends Peter a little. He writes, "No one should wonder that he followed, or cry him up for his manliness. But the wonder was that matter of Peter, that being in such fear, he came even as far as the hall, when others had retreated. His coming thither was caused by love, his not entering within by distress and fear."[4]

3. On the second test the scene could have been in the courtyard of Annas' house, or in a common courtyard shared by Annas and Caiaphas who lived in this general area together. Peter was warming himself at a common outdoor fire when one of the group asked, "Are not you also one of his disciples?" He denied and said, "I am not" (25b, RSV).

4. The next encounter was with a kinsman of Malchus (whose ear Peter had amputated) who said, "Did I not see you in the garden with him?" (26b, RSV). Again Peter denied it. In Mark's account of this scene (and his source was probably Peter himself) he records, "But he began to curse and to swear, saying, I know not this man of whom ye speak" (14:71). It was then that the cock crew for the second time.

In Luke's record of this scene he notes that about this time, "The Lord turned and looked upon Peter" (22:

61a). This broke him up as he recalled the Master's previous warning, so "Peter went out and wept bitterly" (22: 62).

Barclay probes this scene with his comment: "It was the real Peter who protested his loyalty in the Upper Room; it was the real Peter who drew his lonely sword in the moonlight of the garden; it was the real Peter who followed Jesus because he could not leave his Lord alone; it was *not* the real Peter who cracked beneath the tension and who denied his Lord. *And that is just what Jesus could see.*"[5]

Trial Before Pilate (Political)

John 18:28—19:16

28 Then led they Jesus from Caiaphas unto the hall of judgment: and it was early; and they themselves went not into the judgment hall, lest they should be defiled; but that they might eat the passover.
29 Pilate then went out unto them, and said, What accusation bring ye against this man?
30 They answered and said unto him, If he were not a malefactor, we would not have delivered him up unto thee.
31 Then said Pilate unto them, Take ye him, and judge him according to your law. The Jews therefore said unto him, It is not lawful for us to put any man to death:
32 That the saying of Jesus might be fulfilled, which he spake, signifying what death he should die.
33 Then Pilate entered into the judgment hall again, and called Jesus, and said unto him, Art thou the King of the Jews?
34 Jesus answered him, Sayest thou this thing of thyself, or did others tell it thee of me?
35 Pilate answered, Am I a Jew? Thine own nation and the chief priests have delivered thee unto me: what hast thou done?
36 Jesus answered, My kingdom is not of this world: if my kingdom were of this world, then would my servants fight, that I should not be delivered to the Jews: but now is my kingdom not from hence.
37 Pilate therefore said unto him, Art thou a king then? Jesus answered, Thou sayest that I am a king. To this end was I born, and for this cause came I into the world, that I should bear witness unto the truth. Every one that is of the truth heareth my voice.
38 Pilate saith unto him, What is truth? And when he had said this, he he went out again unto the Jews, and saith unto them, I find in him no fault at all.
39 But ye have a custom, that I should release unto you one at the passover: will ye therefore that I release unto you the King of the Jews?
40 Then cried they all again, saying, Not this man, but Barabbas. Now Barabbas was a robber.

19:1 Then Pilate therefore took Jesus, and scourged him.
2 And the soldiers platted a crown of thorns, and put it on his head, and they put on him a purple robe,
3 And said, Hail, King of the Jews! and they smote him with their hands.
4 Pilate therefore went forth again, and saith unto them, Behold, I bring him forth to you, that ye may know that I find no fault in him.
5 Then came Jesus forth, wearing the crown of thorns, and the purple robe. And Pilate saith unto them, Behold the man!
6 When the chief priests therefore and officers saw him, they cried out, saying, Crucify him, crucify him, Pilate saith unto them, Take ye him, and crucify him: for I find no fault in him.
7 The Jews answered him, We have a law, and by our law he ought to die, because he made himself the Son of God.
8 When Pilate therefore heard that saying, he was the more afraid;
9 And went again into the judgment hall, and saith unto Jesus, Whence art thou? But Jesus gave him no answer.
10 Then saith Pilate unto him, Speakest thou not unto me? knowest thou not that I have power to crucify thee, and have power to release thee?
11 Jesus answered, Thou couldest have no power at all against me, except it were given thee from above: therefore he that delivered me unto thee hath the greater sin.
12 And from thenceforth Pilate sought to release him: but the Jews cried out, saying, If thou let this man go, thou art not Caesar's friend: whosoever maketh himself a king speaketh against Caesar.
13 When Pilate therefore heard that saying, he brought Jesus forth, and sat down in the judgment seat in a place that is called the Pavement, but in the Hebrew, Gabbatha.
14 And it was the preparation of the passover, and about the sixth hour: and he saith unto the Jews, Behold your King!
15 But they cried out, Away with him, away with him, crucify him. Pilate saith unto them, Shall I crucify your King? The chief priests answered, We have no king but Caesar.
16 Then delivered he him therefore unto them to be crucified. And they took Jesus, and led him away.

John gives a rather full view of the political (Roman) trial of Jesus, for that is the ground on which He met His death, legally. Also, John's account is in contrast to this phase of the Synoptists' record. They deal more at length with the confrontation before Caiaphas and the Sanhedrin, especially Matthew. Actually, the Sanhedrin had sentenced Jesus to death; their chief issue now was to do it the Roman way, by crucifixion. For this they needed the governor Pilate's consent. Morgan puts it, "Religion had decided to kill Jesus, and now the civil trial goes forward. We see Jesus no longer in the presence of religion, but of government."[6] Actually, sedition was about the only charge that would justify death by crucifixion, and the strongest complaint that came from the Jews was "blasphemy" against God.

1. From the beginning there seems to be tension, if not animosity, between the Roman governor and the Jewish leaders. It is the Passover season, and the city is overflowing with Jews attending their most sacred festival. Besides, the issue of defilement is always before them because of contamination with Gentiles. Where they went immediately before the festival was important. Actually, the Roman governor, Pilate, lived in the Praetorium in Caesarea (Acts 23:35), but there evidently was some recognized government headquarters in Jerusalem to enable him to carry on legal hearings and decisions.

Jesus was brought (a prisoner) from Caiaphas' hearing into the palace then in use. It was early in the morning. But the Jewish leaders stayed outside the acknowledged headquarters lest they become religiously defiled and thus be unable to partake of the Passover. So Pilate accommodated them and went out to them and asked what the charges were against the man before him. They replied with some acidity, "If this man were not an evildoer, we would not have handed him over" (30, RSV). Pilate answered them in kind, "Take him yourselves and judge him by your own law" (31a, RSV). Then the Jews acknowledged, "It is not lawful for us to put any man to death" (31b, RSV). So it was a capital offense they had in mind, punishable by death!

2. Pilate went back to his headquarters again and questioned Jesus, "Are you the king of the Jews? he asked" (33, NEB). Jesus answered, "Is that your own idea or have others suggested it to you?" (34, NEB). Then with a likely shrug Pilate answered, "Am I a Jew? Your own nation and their chief priests have brought you before me. What have you done?" (35, NEB). Then Jesus replied openly, "My kingdom does not belong to this world. If it did, my followers would be fighting to save me from arrest by the

Jews. My kingly authority comes from elsewhere" (36, NEB).

During this dialogue there is no call on the part of Pilate for an interpreter. Most scholars are inclined to think that as governor Pilate would not likely know Aramaic. Some have guessed that Jesus may have spoken Greek and conversed with Pilate in that language. But this is only conjecture.

Presently the governor returned to the only available opening with, "You are a king, then?" he asked (37a, NEB). "Jesus answered, '"King" is your word. My task is to bear witness to the truth. For this I was born; for this I came into the world, and all who are not deaf to truth listen to my voice'" (37, NEB). Jesus seems to be saying to Pilate, "Whenever you reckon with truth, you will reckon with Me." He might even be confessing that He was the King of Truth! With a tinge of possible cynicism Pilate said, "What is truth?" Bacon's essay *Of Truth* gives the haunting line: "What is truth? said jesting Pilate; and would not stay for an answer."

3. It was at this time that Pilate moved out again to the Jews. "'For my part,' he said, 'I find no case against him. But you have a custom that I release one prisoner for you at Passover. Would you like me to release the king of the Jews?" (38b-39, NEB). Now their clamor arose again: "Not him: we want Barabbas!" (40, NEB). (But this man was a robber, a lawless one). They chose the confirmed brigand and condemned the Ruler of the kingdom of God.

JOHN 19

4. Next Pilate moved to what may have been routine in crucifixion cases, but it could be the governor was looking for some compassion from these very religious Jews; he had Jesus flogged. The soldiers at this point entered into the

game; it was all in a day's work; they plaited a crown of thorns and put it on His head. Then they dressed Him up with a purple robe and taunted Him with, "Hail, King of the Jews!" To add venom to their bitterness they slapped Him in the face. What sadistic pleasure they had with the Son of God who had become Son of Man and was about to offer His life for the world's redemption!

5. Pilate went outside to the Jews again and said (for the second time): "Here he is; I am bringing him out to let you know that I find no case against him" (4, NEB). Then he presented Jesus with the introduction, "Behold the Man!" When they say Him, the chief priests and their henchmen shouted, "Crucify! Crucify!" For the third time Pilate said, "I have no case against him" and suggested, "Take him and crucify him yourselves" (6, NEB). "The Jews answered, 'We have a law; and by that law he ought to die, because he has claimed to be the Son of God'" (7, NEB).

Pilate had smoked them out and they offered their true reason for clamoring for Jesus' death. But it made Pilate more afraid than ever, so he took Jesus back to headquarters and quizzed Him one more time. "He asked Jesus, 'Where have you come from?'" (9, NEB). Jesus' answer was majestic silence. "'Do you refuse to speak to me?' said Pilate. 'Surely you know that I have authority to release you, and I have authority to crucify you?' 'You would have no authority at all over me', Jesus replied, 'if it had not been granted you from above; and therefore the deeper guilt lies with the man who handed me over to you'" (10-11, NEB). There is no doubt that Jesus is here referring to Caiaphas, the high priest.

6. It was then that Pilate tried hard to release Jesus, but his own past life haunted him in the endeavor. "The Jews kept shouting, 'If you let this man go, you are no friend to Caesar; any man who claims to be a king is defying Caesar'" (12, NEB). As soon as Pilate discerned what they were saying he moved his court out "and took his seat on

the tribunal at the place known as 'The Pavement'" (13, NEB).

Now it was the eve of the Passover, about noontime. "Pilate said to the Jews, 'Here is your King'" (14*b*, NEB). But it only infuriated them and "they shouted, 'Away with him! Away with him! Crucify him!'" Pilate pressed them still further with, "Crucify your king?" They rejoined, "We have no king but Caesar" (15, NEB). Pilate had brought them low, even in his own defeat. But Pilate's own record could not withstand any further imperial scrutiny. He gave in. "Then at last, to satisfy them he handed Jesus over to be crucified" (16, NEB).

Some years later Paul wrote to his son in the gospel, Timothy, and reminded him that "Christ Jesus . . . in his testimony before Pontius Pilate made the good confession" (1 Tim. 6:13, RSV).

Pilate actually ordered Jesus' scourging even while he professed openly three times that he had acquitted Jesus.

7. He was mocked with royal pomp. The Praetorium was the Roman procurator's official residence at Jerusalem, to which he came, from his normal residence at Caesarea on the coast, in order to prevent disturbances during the Jewish festivals. It was from this place that Pilate gave in. This made Jesus' crucifixion possible—and they had done it legally now, in a Roman court.

The Crucifixion

John 19:17-37

> 17 And he bearing his cross went forth into a place called the place of a skull, which is called in the Hebrew Golgotha:
> 18 Where they crucified him, and two other with him, on either side one, and Jesus in the midst.
> 19 and Pilate wrote a title, and put it on the cross. And the writing was, JESUS OF NAZARETH THE KING OF THE JEWS.
> 20 This title then read many of the Jews: for the place where Jesus was crucified was nigh to the city: and it was written in Hebrew, and Greek, and Latin.
> 21 Then said the chief priests of the Jews to Pilate, Write not, The King of the Jews; but that he said, I am King of the Jews.

22 Pilate answered, What I have written I have written.

23 Then the soldiers, when they had crucified Jesus, took his garments, and made four parts, to every soldier a part; and also his coat: now the coat was without seam, woven from the top throughout.

24 They said therefore among themselves, Let us not rend it, but cast lots for it, whose it shall be: that the scripture might be fulfilled, which saith, They parted my raiment among them, and for my vesture they did cast lots. These things therefore the soldiers did.

25 Now there stood by the cross of Jesus his mother, and his mother's sister, Mary the wife of Cleophas, and Mary Magdalene.

26 When Jesus therefore saw his mother, and the disciple standing by, whom he loved, he saith unto his mother, Woman, behold thy son!

27 Then saith he to the disciple, Behold thy mother! And from that hour that disciple took her unto his own home.

28 After this, Jesus knowing that all things were now accomplished, that the scripture might be fulfilled, saith, I thirst.

29 Now there was set a vessel full of vinegar: and they filled a spunge with vinegar, and put it upon hyssop, and put it to his mouth.

30 When Jesus therefore had received the vinegar, he said, It is finished: and he bowed his head, and gave up the ghost.

31 The Jews therefore, because it was the preparation, that the bodies should not remain upon the cross on the sabbath day, (for that sabbath day was an high day,) besought Pilate that their legs might be broken, and that they might be taken away.

32 Then came the soldiers, and brake the legs of the first, and of the other which was crucified with him.

33 But when they came to Jesus, and saw that he was dead already, they brake not his legs:

34 But one of the soldiers with a spear pierced his side, and forthwith came there out blood and water.

35 And he that saw it bare record, and his record is true: and he knoweth that he saith true, that ye might believe.

36 For these things were done, that the scripture should be fulfilled, A bone of him shall not be broken.

37 And again another scripture saith, They shall look on him whom they pierced.

The Jews had accomplished their real intention with regard to Jesus, namely, to have Him crucified by the Romans, and they did this on the grounds that Jesus claimed to be a king. They insinuated that because of this fact He must be a revolutionary and therefore anti-Roman. Pilate's private talks with Jesus did not bear out these inferences. But in the appointed death on a cross we discover the fulfillment of Jesus' prophetic utterances that He must be lifted up from the earth upon a cross. (See John 3:14; 8:28; 12:32.) Thus His foes and a corrupt government combine to fulfill the divine promise afforded by His redemptive mission.

It was ironical, however, that the Jews—with all

their technical preparations for the passover invading their schedule—do not hesitate to take a confirmed brigand as a released prisoner rather than the Galilean. Their hatred was deep, fundamental, and abiding.

1. None of the Gospel writers dwell very long on the "gory" side of Jesus' death by crucifixion. It was in ordinary circumstances a slow and cruel death. It was indeed capital punishment. The record by John is simple and devastating: "So they took Jesus, and he went out, bearing his own cross, to the place they called the place of a skull, which is called in Hebrew Golgotha. There they crucified him, and with him two others, one on either side, and Jesus between them" (17-18, RSV). It must have looked like "guilt by association" to many of the Jews.

Luke records that one of the thieves taunted Jesus as the trio hung on their respective crosses with, "Are you not the Christ? Save yourself and us!" But the other thief rebuked the insolent one with, "Do you not fear God, since you are under the same sentence of condemnation? And we indeed justly; for we are receiving the due reward of our deeds; but this man hath done nothing wrong" (23:39-41, RSV). Then the second thief added contritely, "Jesus, remember me when you come in your kingly power" (23:42, RSV). With a swiftness that matched His gentleness and assurance Jesus replied, "Truly, I say to you, today you will be with me in Paradise" (23:43, RSV).

Think of it, in the weakest moment of His life Jesus portrayed His redemptive mission clear enough that a brigand could detect a kingdom that could not be destroyed by men and prayed for consideration! The reassurance that Jesus proferred that man still staggers us! Augustine's comment on this scene is majestic and prophetic: "One dying thief was saved so that no one would despair; but only one so that no one would presume."

2. As was the custom, Governor Pilate wrote the title to be placed on Jesus' cross that would identify the prisoner and his capital crime. It read: "Jesus of Nazareth, the King of

the Jews." This description was written in Hebrew, Latin, and Greek. Hebrew was the national language of the Jews; Latin was the language of the government; and Greek was the cultural language of the Mediterranean area. Everyone would be able to read it. Immediately the chief priests objected to Pilate's assigned title and sought to amend it by addition, "This man said, I am the King of the Jews." But Pilate answered them tartly and with finality: "What I have written I have written" (22).

3. Four soldiers carried out the assignment to crucify those three condemned men that day. These soldiers were known as a quaternion. One of the extras they received for this ugly business was they were allowed to keep the clothes of the victims. In Jesus' case they sorted things out and cast lots for His seamless tunic. The Psalmist had written:

"They divided my garments among them,
and for my raiment they cast lots" (22:18, RSV).

Who knows, it could have been His own mother's skilled hands that made that tunic!

4. Simon of Cyrene, Africa, had helped Jesus carry His cross when He needed the lift. The scourging had taken its toll and the much fasting and prayer may have weakened His normal physical reserves. But the real load was the deeper burden of our sins—yours and mine—all alone, at Calvary. A faithful group of women were there, even when nearly all of the inner circle had gone. Who said these were "weaker vessels"? John identifies four: (1) Mary, the mother of Jesus; (2) Salome, sister of Mary and mother of John, the beloved disciple; (3) Mary, the wife of Cleopas; and (4) Mary Magdalene.

Of all of these probably Mary His mother suffered most. She has now realized the fulfillment of Simeon's prophecy in the temple, "And a sword will pierce through your own soul also" (Luke 2:35, RSV). But Jesus was still conscious of her need rather than caring over His own pain, and when He saw John standing near, said to His mother, "Woman, behold, your son!" (John 19:26, RSV). Then He addressed that disciple nearby saying, "Behold your mother!" (27, RSV). The record concludes, "And from that hour the disciple took her to his own home" *(Ibid.).*

Morgan comments here: "He in the midst of the unfathomable things, in the midst of those hours when all the Divine compassions were toiling to redeem men, and exhibit the everlasting mercy, His heart thought about His Mother, and He provided for her for the rest of her earthly pilgrimage."[7] Jesus actually reinforced John by asking him to care for His mother, and by inference, He made His mother strong by allowing her to take John into her affections in a special way. Their mutual exchange of self-giving saved them from the slow burn of self-pity.

Then John's Gospel brings that dark picture to a close. With the full awareness that "all was now finished" Jesus said, "I thirst." It was probably a soldier that responded, for they were in charge, put a sponge in vinegar and put it on a branch or spear and put it to His mouth. John writes, "When Jesus had received the vinegar, he said, 'It is finished'; and he bowed his head and gave up his spirit" (30, RSV). A 19th-century hymn fits this scene.

> *Beneath the cross of Jesus*
> *I fain would take my stand,*
> *The shadow of a mighty rock*
> *Within a weary land;*
> *A home within the wilderness;*
> *A rest upon the way,*
> *From the burning of the noontide heat*
> *And the burden of the day.*
>
> *Upon the cross of Jesus*
> *My eyes at times can see*
> *The very dying form of One*
> *Who suffered there for me.*
> *And from my smitten heart, with tears,*
> *These wonders I confess:*

The wonder of His glorious love,
And my unworthiness.

I take, O Cross, thy shadow
For my abiding place
I ask no other sunshine than
The sunshine of His face;
Content to let the world go by,
To know no gain or loss,
My sinful self my only shame,
My glory all the Cross.

—ELIZABETH C. CLEPHANE

5. Finally the body of Jesus must be removed. He died on the eve of the Passover. Now the Jews were very anxious that the bodies of these three on crosses should not remain there (as the custom was among the Romans, to be an example to the people who passed by). According to Jewish Law the dead body of an executed criminal was not to remain all night "upon the tree," but was to be buried, lest it "defile the land." But this was more especially true when the next day was the Sabbath, and now doubly important because the Sabbath before them was the Passover.

Morris points up the irony of this situation: "The Jews did not want their land defiled by the dead, but they were not concerned that they were themselves defiled by their deed."[8] The Jews then made their special request of Pilate, the governor, that the legs of these criminals be broken to hasten their death. Evidently Pilate gave his approval, for the soldiers broke the legs of Jesus' fellow victims. Upon examination they learned that Jesus was already dead, so one of the soldiers "pierced his side with a spear, and at once there came out blood and water" (34, RSV). John identifies himself as an eyewitness to this detail (35, RSV). John also revels in the fact that "not a bone of him shall be broken"—this, too, was previously foretold and promised (36, RSV).

His Burial

John 19:38-42

> 38 And after this Joseph of Arimathaea, being a disciple of Jesus, but secretly for fear of the Jews, besought Pilate that he might take away the body of Jesus: and Pilate gave him leave. He came therefore, and took the body of Jesus.
> 39 And there came also Nicodemus, which at the first came to Jesus by night, and brought a mixture of myrrh and aloes, about an hundred pound weight.
> 40 Then took they the body of Jesus, and wound it in linen clothes with the spices, as the manner of the Jews is to bury.
> 41 Now in the place where he was crucified there was a garden; and in the garden a new sepulchre, wherein was never man yet laid.
> 42 There laid they Jesus therefore because of the Jews' preparation day; for the sepulchre was nigh at hand.

1. It was fitting that two secret disciples should come out in the open for Jesus on His death. Their courageous front afforded some dignity and a restoration of decency toward the Son of Man when so many of the Jews had heaped scorn and indecent taunts and vulgarities when he was a prisoner at the bar. The disciples for the most part had fled. But Joseph of Arimathaea had standing enough to get an audience with Pilate, the governor, and asked for the body of Jesus. His request was granted after the governor had the centurion check to be sure Jesus was actually dead, for Pilate himself could have been hurting some over his own unfairness and cowardice toward the Galilean.

Also Nicodemus got into the act of his own accord and brought a hundred pounds of a sweet mixture of myrrh and aloes for burial purposes. (Their pound was 12 ounces, so that would mean 75 pounds by our reckoning.)

Both of these men were members of the Sanhedrin, and both were wealthy. Their esteem of Jesus rises to the surface as they treat His dead body with utmost respect.

2. Nearby the place of crucifixion was a garden and there Joseph of Arimathaea had a new-made tomb, never used. Perchance he planned it for himself and/or his family. Jesus knew He was to die, but He made no plans for a decent burial place. Joseph and Nicodemus evidently

counted it a joy to show their sorrow and deep loss in what had been done. The opinions of the Jews who had maneuvered Jesus' death no longer harassed them. Joseph gave Jesus his own brand-new tomb either as an emergency measure or a long-term gift. But Jesus didn't need it long; He changed it into a "short-term" loan and gave it back to Joseph (slightly used) with a long-term interest in the Resurrection which He presently afforded to all mankind.

Nicodemus too brought the best for Jesus. He now was worthy of His love and best gifts. It made no difference who knew about it, for the Sanhedrin did not matter.

What had caused the best of Jesus' inner circle to run and hide and meet behind locked doors now caused these two men to acknowledge Jesus as all He claimed to be. But they were puzzled over His death and maybe blamed themselves for their previous timidity and furtive seeking. Now they have improved. Jesus' body received tender care and belated love. Nicodemus had voted against the crowd in their vote of death, but he didn't throw his vote away, for he still cherished his memory.

The Resurrection would soon change the picture again. That triumph would answer the unanswered questions of the minds and hearts of these well-trained Jews. Their sincerity had come through.

The Resurrection

John 20:1—21:25

JOHN 20

The Empty Tomb

John 20:1-10

1 The first day of the week cometh Mary Magdalene early, when it was yet dark, unto the sepulchre, and seeth the stone taken away from the sepulchre.
2 Then she runneth, and cometh to Simon Peter, and to the other disciple, whom Jesus loved, and saith unto them, They have taken away the Lord out of the sepulchre, and we know not where they have laid him.
3 Peter therefore went forth, and that other disciple, and came to the sepulchre.
4 So they ran both together: and the other disciple did outrun Peter, and came first to the sepulchre.
5 And he stooping down, and looking in, saw the linen clothes lying; yet went he not in.
6 Then cometh Simon Peter following him, and went into the sepulchre, and seeth the linen clothes lie,
7 And the napkin, that was about his head, not lying with the linen clothes, but wrapped together in a place by itself.
8 Then went in also that other disciple, which came first to the sepulchre, and he saw, and believed.
9 For as yet they knew not the scripture, that he must rise again from the dead.
10 Then the disciples went away again unto their own home.

1. The resurrection of Jesus Christ from the dead is for us the miracle above all miracles—not excluding the incarnation of Jesus as Son of Man. William Temple insists that "the date of the triumph of love is Good Friday, not Easter

Day."[1] But it was a dark day for the disciples of Jesus when He was crucified, and the light did not shine upon them clearly again until He showed them His hands and His side on their first appointed meeting in a designated area.

a. Even a casual reading of the New Testament record presents the practical question readily to inquiring minds, "What happened to those fearful disciples between the day of Jesus' arrest by the Romans and temple soldiers and their subsequent vibrant and courageous ministry on the day of Pentecost?" All the gospel writers combine to give us two great events that brought about the significant change: (1) Jesus arose from the tomb and presented himself in resurrected, bodily form that was identifiable to them; (2) The Holy Spirit came upon the believing Church in a personal way on the day of Pentecost as they prayed in waiting obedience. This invisible, but nonetheless real, Presence now came upon them in purifying, quickening power and made the difference in their dynamic witness.

b. Temple points out that "St. John does not promote the Resurrection as a mighty act by which the hosts of evil are routed, but rather as the quiet rising of the sun which has already vanquished night."[2] Even after the mighty truth of the resurrection had dawned upon the church they gave their witness to it as something inevitable, based on the person and power of God. Paul's reasoning before Agrippa is a case in point. He asked, "Why is it thought incredible by any of you that God raises the dead?" (Acts 26:8, RSV). Also in Peter's memorable message on the day of Pentecost itself in which he identified himself with Jesus of Nazareth whom the Jews had killed, declared in part: "This Jesus, delivered up according to the definite plan and foreknowledge of God, you crucified and killed by the hands of lawless men. But God raised him up, having loosed the pangs of death, because it was not possible for him to be held by it" (Acts 2:23-24, RSV). In the same general setting, Peter also adds, "And of that we all are witnesses" (2:32). Here the direct reference is to Jesus' resurrection. His total message was his classical and historical explanation of their newfound dynamic witness.

2. John's account of the Resurrection discovery highlights a lone woman, Mary Magdalene. Some Bible students seem surprised and almost shocked that she should be the first to whom Jesus revealed himself as risen Lord. But God does not always do things our way, neither did Jesus seem to perform miracles for show or do them on prime time! Surely there is no chauvinism in God who created us, male and female! Jesus may have revealed himself to Mary Magdalene because she was there and loved Him for himself as well as His redemptive power in her own life. She needed Him and her tears wouldn't dry—so He made her His first appointed witness. She reported to the disciples as instructed, "I have seen the Lord," and gave them His message (18). In Luke's account in which a group of women (including Mary of Magdala) reported to the 11 and all the others concerning the message of the angels, he gives their reaction: "The story appeared to them to be nonsense, and they would not believe them" (24:11, NEB).

It was also in Luke's account that we learn: "The women who had accompanied him from Galilee followed [Joseph of Arimathea and others with the body of Jesus for burial]; they took note of the tomb and observed how his body was laid. Then they went home and prepared spices and perfumes" (23:55-56, NEB).

3. Lightfoot underscores the two main points that John enumerates in his account of the Resurrection. He observes, "The two points on which St. John lays emphasis in his resurrection narrative are, first, the resumption by the Lord of the personal relations and intercourse with those who had followed Him during His ministry and, secondly, the identity of the Lord's risen body with the body which suffered and was laid in the tomb. At His first reunion with the disciples after the Resurrection He shows them His hands and His side (20:20) and, at the second, St. Thomas is invited to satisfy himself absolutely on this

point (20:27)."[3] We must point out, however, that Jesus' visits with His disciples were intermittent and not continuous. This could have been to prepare them for the unbroken leadership of the Holy Spirit following Pentecost.

Lightfoot is also careful to point out that St. John's teaching in chapter 20 is parallel to the sacramental teaching in chapter 6.[4] We would agree with Lightfoot's conclusion that while the Lord's incarnation, death, resurrection, ascension, and bestowal of the Spirit are distinctive events "forming a connected temporal process," these together are also "drawn together into one."[5] They are all part of the economy of grace and must be understood in relation to the whole. This is "the word of faith which we preach" (Rom. 10:8b).

The Appearance to Mary Magdalene

John 20:11-18

> 11 But Mary stood without at the sepulchre weeping: and as she wept, she stooped down, and looked into the sepulchre,
> 12 And seeth two angels in white sitting, the one at the head, and the other at the feet, where the body of Jesus had lain.
> 13 And they say unto her, Woman, why weepest thou? She saith unto them, Because they have taken away my Lord, and I know not where they have laid him.
> 14 And when she had thus said, she turned herself back, and saw Jesus standing, and knew not that it was Jesus.
> 15 Jesus saith unto her, Woman, why weepest thou? whom seekest thou? She, supposing him to be the gardener, saith unto him, Sir, if thou have borne him hence, tell me where thou hast laid him, and I will take him away.
> 16 Jesus saith unto her, Mary. She turned herself, and saith unto him, Rabboni; which is to say, Master.
> 17 Jesus saith unto her, Touch me not; for I am not yet ascended to my Father: but go to my brethren, and say unto them, I ascend unto my Father, and your Father; and to my God, and your God.
> 18 Mary Magdalene came and told the disciples that she had seen the Lord, and that he had spoken these things unto her.

1. Mary Magdalene came to the tomb early on that memorable First Day to do tribute to the memory of the One she loved. She was accompanied by other devoted women, but it could have been that she came before them. Her normal fear of the dark was dissipated by the tragedy and unabated excitement of recent events. She may have ar-

rived as early as 3 a.m. The supreme desire of the total group of women was to complete (as needed) the normal Jewish reverence and tribute to Jesus by treating His body with further spices. The intervening Sabbath had delayed them a bit. What had been done previously was surely done in haste, they thought. Some of them had observed and knew what Joseph of Arimathaea had done, but it could have been they were not fully aware of the generous contribution of spices (myrrh and aloes) made by Nicodemus on that fateful day of Jesus' death and burial.

a. It must have been a horrible shock to Mary of Magdala to note that the stone that blocked the entrance to the tomb had been moved away. Without any delay, Mary ran to find the two men who were closest to Jesus—Peter and John. It is even possible that John had looked up Peter after his own original return from the tomb, for he could well guess that Peter might be "very low" by that time. Even the first oral message later as recorded by Mark, and given to the women at the tomb, was to be delivered to "his disciples and Peter" (16:7).

b. Mary's simple but excited word now was: "They have taken the Lord out of his tomb, and we do not know where they have laid him" (John 20:2*b*, NEB). Mary ran to find these men, so they returned the compliment and ran to the site of the tomb themselves and John came in first. Sure enough, it was just as Mary had reported the situation. John looked in enough to see the cloth wrappings of Jesus, but he did not go in. When Peter got there, he went into the tomb without taking time to get his breath. "He saw the linen wrappings lying, and the napkin which had been over his head, not lying with the wrappings but rolled together in a place by itself" (6-7, NEB). Then John followed Peter. His confession reads: "Then the disciple who had reached the tomb first went in too and he saw and believed" (10, NEB). So John the Apostle heads the list of the early believers among the apostles—even before he saw the Lord for himself! The graveclothes seem to tell him that thieves don't sort things out like that, even at night.

Hoskyns observes here, "The pre-eminence of the faith of the Beloved Disciple is the climax of the narrative."[6]

2. "But Mary stood weeping outside the tomb" (11, RSV), and there is strong likelihood that she was sobbing. Just then she stooped to look into the tomb and "saw two angels in white, sitting where the body of Jesus had lain, one at the head and one at the feet" (12, RSV). They asked why she was weeping and she replied, "Because they have taken away my Lord, and I do not know where they have laid him" (13, RSV).

Lenski observes here, "Indeed, why does she weep when we all have cause to weep to all eternity if what she wept for had been given to her, the dead body of her Lord!"[7] Just then Mary turned and saw Jesus standing, but she did not recognize Him. (She actually guessed he might be the gardener!) She pursued with, "Sir, if you have carried him away, tell me where you have laid him, and I will take him away" (15, RSV). It was then that Jesus called her by name, "Mary."

The accents and the tone were now inescapable. She turned and said to Him in Hebrew, "Rabboni" (16, RSV). Her word really meant "Teacher" or "Master." Then Jesus admonished her not to cling to Him explaining, "For I have not ascended to the Father. But go to my brothers and tell them that I am now ascending to my Father and your Father, my God and your God" (17, NEB). Temple reminds us, "Alike for fulness of our love to Him, and for the fulness of His power working in us, we are to cling, not to the Lord known after the flesh (2 Cor. 5:16) but to the Lord enthroned at the right hand of the Father and active within us by the energy of the Holy Spirit."[8]

Promptly Mary went to the disciples with her news: "I have seen the Lord" (17, NEB). She also delivered the rest of her message. The men didn't believe her or any of the other women's witness. They probably ascribed it to a woman's lively imagination and born of grief!

(See appendix for a sermon outline on John 20:15.)

First Appearance to the Disciples; Thomas Doubts
John 20:19-25

19 Then the same day at evening, being the first day of the week, when the doors were shut where the disciples were assembled for fear of the Jews, came Jesus and stood in the midst, and saith unto them, Peace be unto you.
20 And when he had so said, he shewed unto them his hands and his side. Then were the disciples glad, when they saw the Lord.
21 Then said Jesus to them again, Peace be unto you: as my Father hath sent me, even so send I you.
22 And when he had said this, he breathed on them, and saith unto them, Receive ye the Holy Ghost:
23 Whose soever sins ye remit, they are remitted unto them; and whose soever sins ye retain, they are retained.
24 But Thomas, one of the twelve, called Didymus, was not with them when Jesus came.
25 The other disciples therefore said unto him, We have seen the Lord. But he said unto them, Except I shall see in his hands the print of the nails, and put my finger into the print of the nails, and thrust my hand into his side, I will not believe.

It was late in the evening of the first Easter Day. The meeting probably took place after those who had walked the Emmaus Road with Jesus had returned and reported their visit with Him, and especially the revelation at the breaking of bread. Also, the report had come that Jesus had seen Peter. That night there were only 10 apostles gathered with the company, for Thomas was missing. The doors were locked for fear of the Jews. There was no telling what those leaders who had "rubbed out" Jesus so surely and so legally would do next.

1. The record reads, "Jesus came and stood among them. 'Peace be with you!' he said, and then showed them his hands and his side" (19-20, NEB). John is the only Gospel writer who reports that Jesus showed them His side. Here identity and restoration are confirmed in one confrontation. Then the disciples were filled with joy to overflowing. Jesus repeated His salutation, now with new understanding, "Peace be with you!"

2. At this point Jesus added His commission (as given previously in His high priestly prayer, John 17:18). He now says, "As the Father has sent me, even so send I you"

(20:21, RSV). Next He breathed on them and said to them, "Receive the Holy Spirit. If you forgive the sins of any, they are forgiven; if you retain the sins of any, they are retained" (22-23, RSV). Some have stumbled a bit on this passage, reminding us that the Holy Spirit was not actually bestowed upon the Church until the climactic day of Pentecost. They have also queried on the issue, "Did Jesus actually turn the forgiveness of sins over to the apostles themselves?"

a. Hoskyns explains: "The resurrection scenes in the Fourth Gospel are all preparatory scenes, preparatory for the mission. What the Lord will do invisibly from heaven He here does visibly on earth. The mission is inaugurated, but not actually begun. The disciples still remain in secret, behind closed doors. The actual beginning of the mission lies outside the scope of the Fourth Gospel. There remains, therefore, room for the Pentecostal outpouring."[9] Morris adds: "Their mission proceeds from His. It is only because He has accomplished His mission, and precisely because He accomplished it, that they are sent into the world."[10]

b. Morris points out concerning the forgiveness of sins that these words "apply to the church as a whole and not to individuals."[11] Barclay also explains: "This sentence does not mean that the power to forgive sins is entrusted to any man or to any men, it means that the power to proclaim that forgiveness is so entrusted to them. This sentence lays down the duty of the Church to convey forgiveness to the penitent in heart, and to warn the impenitent that they are forfeiting the mercy of God."[12]

3. Later on, when the disciples told Thomas, "We have seen the Lord," he demurred and insisted, "Unless I see the marks of the nails of his hands, unless I put my finger into the place where the nails were, and my hand into his side, I will not believe" (25, NEB). He demanded to see and feel for himself. He ignored both the number and character of the 10 witnesses. He was stubbornly doubtful.

Low in the grave He lay—Jesus, my Saviour!
Waiting the coming day—Jesus, my Lord!

Vainly they watch His bed—Jesus, my Saviour!
Vainly they seal the dead—Jesus, my Lord!

Death cannot keep his prey—Jesus, my Saviour!
He tore the bars away—Jesus, my Lord!

REFRAIN:
Up from the grave He arose,
With a mighty triumph o'er His foes,
He arose a Victor from the dark domain,
And He lives forever with His saints to reign.
He arose! He arose! Hallelujah! Christ arose!

—ROBERT LOWRY

Second Appearance to the Disciples; Thomas Believes
John 20:26-29

> 26 And after eight days again his disciples were within, and Thomas with them: then came Jesus, the doors being shut, and stood in the midst, and said, Peace be unto you.
> 27 Then saith he to Thomas, Reach hither thy finger, and behold my hands; and reach hither thy hand, and thrust it into my side: and be not faithless, but believing.
> 28 And Thomas answered and said unto him, My Lord and my God.
> 29 Jesus saith unto him, Thomas, because thou hast seen me, thou hast believed: blessed are they that have not seen, and yet have believed.

In the second appearance to His disciples, Jesus indulged Thomas, the Twin, a little. Thomas had demanded both sight and touch to convince him that Jesus had risen from the dead. It was exactly a week later from His first visit to the group that Jesus reappeared. It was evidently largely for Thomas' benefit. They met in the same room with essentially the same group. Jesus' salutation was the same as before. Then he addressed Thomas personally, "Reach your finger: see my hands; be unbelieving no longer, but believe" (27, NEB). Thomas was overwhelmed; the sight of Jesus caused him to withdraw his tactile demands and brought forth with much feeling, "My Lord and my God!" (28, NEB). Now Thomas has made the greatest confession of all, for he has acknowledged that Jesus is God. Immediately Jesus responded, "Because you have seen me you have found faith. Happy [blessed] are they who never saw me and yet have found faith" (29, NEB). G. Campbell Morgan calls this, "His [Jesus'] last beatitude."[13]

Jesus had prayed in His high priestly prayer and remembered His disciples in a special way, but He also encompassed within His reach "those who believe on me through their word" (John 17:20). Later on, Paul wrote a letter declaring, "We conclude that faith is awakened by the message, and the message that awakens it comes through the word of Christ" (Rom. 10:17, NEB).

Faith is a divine gift, but it is also a task on our part.

Motive for Writing the Gospel

John 20:30-31

> 30 And many other signs truly did Jesus in the presence of his disciples, which are not written in this book:
> 31 But these are written, that ye might believe that Jesus is the Christ, the Son of God; and that believing ye might have life through his name.

John here acknowledges that he has made a selection of events and messages given. His story has not been intended to be exhaustive. John acknowledges that the disciples themselves were witnesses to the events recorded. It does not assume that all of them witnessed every scene. Actually, John seems to underscore the scenes where he was likely to have been a witness. His "inner circle" position among the Twelve made this readily possible.

John also owns up to his frankly evangelistic purpose, for this was his own mission as an apostle. He is not a propagandist in the usual sense, but the message of the Christian faith is his basic motive for writing.

We rather think that John also wrote in several situations to supplement what had already been written by others, and it could be that he wrote at times to correct some mistaken notion that had arisen out of widespread oral tradition.

For John, Jesus is the long-expected One, but He is also the unique Son of God. But John also wants to see the faith that accepted Jesus for who He is perpetuated in their daily lives. Morris agrees that "faith is an adventure which must be renewed each day, and even that John's words may be used with profit by those who are already Christians."[14]

JOHN 21

The Final Appearance in Galilee

John 21:1-14

> 1 After these things Jesus shewed himself again to the disciples at the sea of Tiberias; and on this wise shewed he himself.
> 2 There were together Simon Peter, and Thomas called Didymus, and Nathanael of Cana in Galilee, and the sons of Zebedee, and two other of his disciples.
> 3 Simon Peter saith unto them, I go a fishing. They say unto him, We also go with thee. They went forth, and entered into a ship immediately: and that night they caught nothing.
> 4 But when the morning was now come, Jesus stood on the shore: but the disciples knew not that it was Jesus.
> 5 Then Jesus saith unto them, Children, have ye any meat? They answered him, No.
> 6 And he said unto them, Cast the net on the right side of the ship, and ye shall find. They cast therefore, and now they were not able to draw it for the multitude of fishes.
> 7 Therefore that disciple whom Jesus loved saith unto Peter, it is the Lord. Now when Simon Peter heard that it was the Lord, he girt his fisher's coat unto him, (for he was naked,) and did cast himself into the sea.
> 8 And the other disciples came in a little ship; (for they were not far from land, but as it were two hundred cubits,) dragging the net with fishes.
> 9 As soon then as they were come to land, they saw a fire of coals there, and fish laid thereon, and bread.
> 10 Jesus saith unto them, Bring of the fish which ye have now caught.
> 11 Simon Peter went up, and drew the net to land full of great fishes, an hundred and fifty and three: and for all there were so many, yet was not the net broken.

12 Jesus saith unto them, Come and dine. And none of the disciples durst ask him, Who art thou? knowing that it was the Lord.
13 Jesus then cometh, and taketh bread, and giveth them, and fish likewise.
14 This is now the third time that Jesus shewed himself to his disciples, after that he was risen from the dead.

This chapter reads like an addendum following chapter 20. But it is a charming story of Jesus' probing of Peter and His recommissioning him to care for the flock of God. The chapter itself divides readily into two parts: (1) The fishing expedition which rallied seven disciples, led by Simon Peter, on the sea of Tiberias; and (2) The scene involving the open restoration and semi-public commissioning of Peter for his life's work, and a general forecast of John's future.

1. We don't know why Peter got up the fishing expedition. Their funds may have been depleted and their food supplies low. Or, there could have been an unsettled feeling of transition upon them as Jesus appeared and disappeared throughout that post-Resurrection period prior to Pentecost. Originally (according to Matthew's account and Mark's report) Jesus had said to two pairs of brothers: "Follow me, and I will make you fishers of men." They promptly left their nets and their business and followed Him.

   a. Now there seems to be a vacuum, or something akin to it. Peter proposed the trip and six others fell in with him; no dissent so far as we can detect. This was their self-chosen profession, and it was best done at night. Their former skills had not left them, but that night they caught nothing. This had probably happened to them in the former days of fishing, but now it was different.

   As the dawn broke upon them they could see Someone on the shore. He called out to the fishermen, "Friends, have you caught anything?" (5, NEB). Their answer was No. The Stranger said, "Cast the net on the right side [starboard] of the boat, and you will find some" (6, RSV). Immediately they caught a haul of fish so great that they could not pull them aboard the boat. It was then that John turned to Peter and said quickly, "It is the Lord!" Promptly Peter wrapped his coat about him and plunged into the sea, for he had been operating fisherman's style—stripped for work. The others stayed on board and dragged the fish-laden net to the shore. They were then only about 100 yards from the land.

b. When they came ashore they found that the Master himself was their chef but nobody asked, "Who are You?" They knew. He had a live charcoal fire with fish cooking, and bread. Jesus suggested, "Bring some of your catch" (10, NEB). Presently He gave the call, "Come and have breakfast." Then Jesus served them bread and fish. What a meal! What a Chef! What a Waiter!

"This makes the third time that Jesus appeared to his disciples after his resurrection from the dead" (14, NEB).

The Commission to Peter and to John

John 21:15-23

15 So when they had dined, Jesus saith to Simon Peter, Simon, son of Jonas, lovest thou me more than these? He saith unto him, Yea, Lord; thou knowest that I love thee. He saith unto him, Feed my lambs.
16 He saith to him again the second time, Simon, son of Jonas, lovest thou me? He saith unto him, Yea, Lord; thou knowest that I love thee. He saith unto him, Feed my sheep.
17 He saith unto him the third time, Simon, son of Jonas, lovest thou me? Peter was grieved because he said unto him the third time, Lovest thou me? And he said unto him, Lord, thou knowest all things; thou knowest that I love thee. Jesus saith unto him, Feed my sheep.
18 Verily, verily, I say unto thee, When thou wast young, thou girdedst thyself, and walkedst whither thou wouldest: but when thou shalt be old, thou shalt stretch forth thy hands, and another shall gird thee, and carry thee whither thou wouldest not.
19 This spake he, signifying by what death he should glorify God. And when he had spoken this, he saith unto him, Follow me.
20 Then Peter, turning about, seeth the disciple whom Jesus loved following; which also leaned on his breast at supper, and said, Lord, which is he that betrayeth thee?
21 Peter seeing him saith to Jesus, Lord, and what shall this man do?
22 Jesus saith unto him, If I will that he tarry till I come, what is that to thee? follow thou me.
23 Then went this saying abroad among the brethren, that that disciple should not die: yet Jesus said not unto him, He shall not die; but, If I will that he tarry till I come, what is that to thee?

In his initial call to follow Jesus, Simon Peter was brought by his brother Andrew. The latter said to his brother, "'We have found the Messiah' (which is Hebrew for Christ)" (John 1:41, NEB). When Jesus confronted Simon, He "looked him in the face, and said, 'You are Simon, son of John. You shall be called Cephas' (that is, Peter the Rock)" (1:42, NEB). It was after this that Jesus challenged Peter with others, to follow Him and He would make them "fishers of men."

1. Peter proved to be a leader from the first. Sometimes he was a bit brash, and on occasion did not hesitate to argue with His Lord. At one period when some of Jesus' followers were dropping out, Jesus asked the Twelve, "Do you also want to leave me?" (6:67, NEB). Peter's comeback was quick and enthusiastic, "Lord, to whom shall we go? Your words are words of eternal life. We have faith, and we know that you are the Holy One of God" (6:68-69, NEB).

a. Jesus did not frequently spend time probing His own image, but it was at Caesarea Philippi that He asked His disciples outright, "But who do you say that the Son of Man is?" Simon Peter replied, "You are the Christ [Messiah], the Son of the living God" (Matt. 16:15-16, RSV). Jesus immediately commended him with, "Blessed are you Simon Bar Jona! For flesh and blood has not revealed this to you, but my Father who is in heaven" (v. 17, RSV).

b. But when Jesus began to prepare His inner circle for the Cross that was soon to be upon Him, and to assure them of His resurrection in three days afterward, Peter took Him to one side "and began to rebuke him, saying, "Be it far from thee, Lord: this shall not be unto thee" (Matt. 16:22). Promptly "Jesus turned and said to Peter, 'Away with you, Satan; you are a stumbling-block to me. You think as men think, not as God thinks'" (v. 23, NEB). The wise man had observed long before, "Faithful are the wounds of a friend; but the kisses of an enemy are deceitful" (Prov. 27:5).

c. It was just before the last journey into Jerusalem that Peter had blurted out, "Lo, we have left everything and followed you" (Mark 10:28). Jesus' answer was that they should "receive in this age a hundred times as much —houses, brothers and sisters, mothers and children and land—and persecutions besides; and in the age to come eternal life" (Mark 10:30, NEB).

d. In a protesting mood near the close, Peter raised a question over the propriety of his Master washing his feet. When Jesus came to him, Peter said, "'You, Lord washing my feet?' Jesus replied, 'You do not understand now what I am doing, but one day you will'" (John 13:6-7, NEB). But this did not change Peter's view for he insisted, "I will never let you wash my feet" (v. 8, NEB). Jesus' answer was equally firm: "If I do not wash you, you are not in fellowship with me" *(ibid.).* Then Peter caved in and went to the extreme the other way—again arguing with Jesus— "Not my feet only; wash my hands and head as well!" (v. 9, NEB).

e. When it came to Jesus' arrest in the garden the disciples carried two swords; Peter had one of them and used it on Malchus, the servant of the high priest, cutting off his ear. Jesus healed the ear and prevented real panic.

2. The present scene before us is the restoration of this man, Peter, initially the leading apostle. He had failed badly when he denied his Lord, despite the Master's warning. But Jesus looked tenderly at Peter and his tears that followed were bitter with penitence. Also, the Resurrection message from the young man in white to the disciples included, "Go your way, tell his disciples and Peter that he goeth before you into Galilee: there shall ye see him, as he said unto you" (Mark 16:7). The scriptures also reveal that Jesus appeared separately to Peter himself, but no account of the conversations of that meeting is recorded.

a. What a setting Jesus afforded Peter for this encounter! He prepared a meal (par excellence) himself for the entire fishing party and served it with humility, love, tenderness, and compassion. Then after breakfast, He moved in with that serious question to Peter, "Simon son of John, do you love me more than all else?" (15, NEB). Peter's answer was, "Yes, Lord, you know that I love you." Jesus' rejoinder was, "Then feed my lambs" *(ibid.)*. Twice more Jesus asked Peter if he loved Him and by now the query "reached" Peter that Jesus had asked him *three times*. He seemed grieved or hurt by the coincidence with his three denials. On his third reply of yes, Peter added, "Lord you know everything; you know that I love you" (17, NEB). To each of his replies Jesus responded with a challenge to feed or guide the flock of God.

b. Then Jesus spoke with reassurance concerning Peter's future service. He said: "Further, I tell you this in very truth: when you were young you fastened your belt about you and walked where you chose; but when you are old you will stretch out your arms, and a stranger will bind you fast, and carry you where you have no wish to go" (18, NEB). John explains that Jesus was indicating the manner of Peter's death that was to glorify God. Then Jesus added, "Follow me."

c. Just at that moment, as John followed Jesus and Peter, the latter asked the Master, "Lord, what will happen to him?" (21, NEB). But Jesus' reply was simply, "If it should be my will that he wait until I come, what is it to you?" (22, NEB). Jesus said this to Peter, but his answer here is good for all of us when we are asking curious or impertinent questions that are too casual.

d. John Wesley (in his notes on the New Testament) estimates that Peter lived about 36 years after this. John probably lived to a ripe old age. Tradition has it that Peter was actually crucified as his Lord, and one version reports that he insisted on being crucified upside down because he was not worthy of an identical crucifixion as his Lord. But Peter's final record was good; he did not fail his Lord.

His mature outlook on life is well portrayed in his First Epistle to the scattered churches. Its philosophy was hammered out on the anvil of experience: "Now who is there to harm you if you are zealous for what is right? But even if you do suffer for righteousness' sake you will be blessed. Have no fear of them, nor be troubled, but in your hearts reverence Christ as Lord" (1 Pet. 3:13-15, RSV).

> *Jesus calls us; o'er the tumult*
> *Of our life's wild, restless sea,*
> *Day by day His sweet voice soundeth,*
> *Saying, "Christian, follow Me."*
>
> *Jesus calls us from the worship*
> *Of the vain world's golden store,*
> *From each idol that would keep us,*
> *Saying, "Christian, love me more."*
>
> *In our joys and in our sorrows,*
> *Days of toil and hours of ease,*
> *Still He calls, in cares and pleasures,*
> *"Christian, love Me more than these."*
>
> *Jesus calls us. By Thy mercies,*
> *Saviour, may we hear Thy call,*
> *Give our hearts to Thy obedience,*
> *Serve and love Thee best of all.*
> —CECIL F. ALEXANDER

Concluding Notes

John 21:24-25

> 24 This is the disciple which testifieth of these things, and wrote these things: and we know that his testimony is true.
> 25 And there are also many other things which Jesus did, the which, if they should be written every one, I suppose that even the world itself could not contain the books that should be written. Amen.

These concluding words identify the disciple mentioned as the one referred to throughout as "the disciple whom Jesus loved," namely John. As usual, John does not name himself or even his family throughout the gospel. But the intent of these two verses (with their immediate context) seems to identify John as the author and source of this gospel. Throughout the entire book there is an authentic, eyewitness ring and a personal understanding of geography, customs, and people. Above all, he seems to know Jesus as an intimate disciple of His. John's main goal and motive is that men might believe on His name. This is the clue to humanity's aim for eternal life (John 17: 3).

John admits that his task seems to be unending in action, depth, and implications. This is the key to his hyperbole. He also may be including the entire witnessing church in his "we" of verse 24 and indicates that they did corroborate his testimony. This, too, leads us to think that John wrote clearly and with assurance, and probably a bit earlier than some able scholars would have guessed half a century ago.

We close with the NEB translation of the last two verses (24-25).

"It is this same disciple who attests what has here been written. It is in fact he who wrote it, and we know that his testimony is true.

"There is much else that Jesus did. If it were all to be recorded in detail, I suppose the whole world would not hold the books that would be written."

> Tell me the old, old story
>   Of unseen things above,
> Of Jesus and His glory,
>   Of Jesus and His love,
> Tell me the story simply,
>   As to a little child;
> For I am weak and weary,
>   And helpless and defiled.
>
> Tell me the story slowly,
>   That I may take it in—

That wonderful redemption,
  God's remedy for sin.
Tell me the story often,
  For I forget so soon.
The "early dew" of morning
  Has passed away at noon.

Tell me the same old story
  When you have cause to fear
That this world's empty glory
  Is costing me too dear.
Yes, and when that world's glory
  Is dawning on my soul,
Tell me the old, old story:
  "Christ Jesus makes thee whole."
                    —KATHERINE HANKEY

Appendix

Outlines for Sermons from the Gospel of John

The Clarity of a Divine Mission

TEXT: John 6:6

*This he said to prove him: for he himself knew what
he would do.*

1. *The motivation was divine love*
   a. It was a *prime* motivation and not a personal success formula.
   b. He was "moved with compassion."
2. *His style had a charming simplicity*
   a. To meet a need; they had traveled far by foot to hear him.
   b. He used a lad's lunch; what was available.
   c. He blessed it by prayer and it multiplied.
   d. Organized them into companies to prevent chaos.
3. *Discernment accompanies obedience to the Father's will*
   a. He involves His apostles in service.
   b. The Father sanctifies the boy's gift of all he had with him.
   c. No scrambling for superior portions, "Labor not for the meat that perisheth" (v. 27).
   d. Was aware of His Father's resources.
4. *Conservation method applied*
   a. A part of stewardship
   b. What is ours came from God
   c. "Little is much when God is in it"; but even the little belongs to Him. He trusts us.

The Approach to Truth

TEXT: John 7:17

*If any man will do his will, he shall know of the
doctrine.*

Introduction:
1. In Jesus' use of this passage, He used it as a formula that doubters might use to examine the validity of His message and authority.
2. We may use it to reexamine our own integrity in following the truth of God.
3. In the Prologue, John wrote: "The true light [Jesus] that enlightens every man was coming into the world" (1:9, RSV).

A. *Light by an Intuitive Flash Sometimes Comes to Us from God*
   1. Moses by the burning bush (Exod. 3:1-17). When he paid attention, God spoke.
      a. Called him by name
      b. Afforded great worship in a humble wilderness shrine
      c. "I will send you"—His commission
   2. Isaiah (6:1-9)—the vision of God, high and exalted
      a. His confession
         (1) For himself
         (2) For his people
      b. The moral character of God changes everything
      c. Mission offered and accepted
   3. Saul of Tarsus—on Damascus road
      a. Saw the light flash (Acts 9:3-6)
      b. His name called
      c. His questions:
         (1) Who art thou? (*Ans.:* Jesus whom thou persecutest)
         (2) What wilt thou have me to do? (*Ans.:* Arise and go into the city and it shall be told you what to do next.)

B. *The Ethical Approach to the Way*

   1. Follow the gleam

   2. Obey instructions:
     a. Begin where you know
     b. Light brightens as steps are taken

   3. How de we know it is God?
     a. By His demands
     b. By the moral tone of His direction
     c. His commands involve corresponding promises. Wesley: "God's commands are only covered promises."

C. *Life Is a Combination of the Above*

   1. Saul of Tarsus
     a. God had prepared Ananias
     b. His blindness cured
     c. Subsequently God afforded him Barnabas as an elder brother

   2. Moses' instructions were confirmed as he responded.
     a. Don't seek for skywriting; He has given us His Word
     b. Stunts feed unbelief and pride.

   3. Jesus guarantees that God's insights are open to anyone who is willing to do His will (John 1:17).

   4. Practical obedience involves faith, and conversely faith demands response in life.
     a. Trust and obey go together.
     b. Augustine declared: "Understanding is the reward of faith. Therefore do not seek to understand in order to believe, but believe that thou mayest understand."
     c. Stand on the promises of God. Faith is both a gift and a task. "Faith cometh by hearing, and hearing by the word of God" (Rom. 10:17).

The Holy Spirit Promised

TEXT: John 7:37-39

*If any man thirst, let him come unto me, and drink.
He that believeth on me, as the scripture hath said,
out of his belly shall flow rivers of living water. (But
this spake he of the Spirit, which they that believe on
him should receive: for the Holy Ghost was not yet
given; because that Jesus was not yet glorified.)*

Introduction:

1. The poverty of human language in describing spiritual truth (a symbolic language).

    Have you ever tried to describe the taste of water? Try it in 50 to 100 words sometime. We have had college students tell us it tasted "wet." One good student declared it tasted like milk, only different. But how do you describe it?

2. John the apostle gives us the true exegesis of this passage (v. 39, RSV).

    The disciples were instructed to "wait for the promise of the Father"—the coming of the Holy Spirit. (Read Acts 1:4-8.)

3. John the Baptist had identified this as Jesus' special baptism. (See Luke 3:16-17.)

A. *A Fundamental Need Met*

1. As described by water
    a. Normal—as fundamental as water
    b. Not simply ecstacy

2. Water speaks of cleansing
    Inner condition—a fountain of living—pure—reliable—healthy water

3. Meets our inner need ("inmost being")

4. Water speaks here of overflow
    Divine adequacy
    Rivers describe the torrential supply

B. *Afforded by God Alone*

    1. Through Jesus Christ
       "Come to me"

    2. Through faith in Jesus, the Meritorious Cause for
       our salvation
       The invitation is to "drink"

    3. The Fountainhead is God, through the Holy Spirit
       He comes as a gift.

C. *An Inward Experience*

    1. Out of our inner life
       John 7:38*b* (RSV) "Out of his heart shall flow
       rivers of living water."
       "Out from within . . . shall flow" (NEB)
       "Flowing from his inmost heart" (Phillips)

    2. It never runs dry
       God, by His Holy Spirit, is the Source and true
       Fountainhead.

    3. Was first realized at Pentecost
       Even there the promise was to all that are afar
       off.

    4. No discrimination—"If anyone thirst"
       a. In the divine call—"Come to me"
       b. In the divine answer—God does not tantalize

    5. Faith must be present tense
       a. One prayed—"The Holy Spirit for me now"
       b. Immediacy an element of faith—*now* I believe

The Extravagance of Love

Text: John 12:3

*Then took Mary a pound of ointment of spikenard,
very costly, and anointed the feet of Jesus, and wiped
his feet with her hair: and the house was filled with
the odour of the ointment.*

Introduction:
1. What constitutes unreasonable or excessive spending?
2. Does love know ready limits at home?
    a. Mother—child
    b. Parents for disabled one
    c. The Prodigal Father's welcome of son (Luke 15: 22-24, 32)

A. *Love's Extravagance in the Gift of God's Son*
1. John 3:16 becomes the measure of the Father's love.
2. The motive in John 3:17
    a. Constancy—John 17:4; mission accomplished
    b. The same in-depth view—John 8:28-29

B. *Mary's Extravagance Justified*
1. The raising of Lazarus
    a. He had been dead and buried
    b. Resurrection power exemplified
       Lazarus home again—at table with Jesus
2. The sadness in Jesus' eyes as He sees the Cross loom up before Him.
    a. Nothing too costly for Him
    b. Mary already rejoiced in what she had done.
    c. Her gift gave her perspective and a sense of values.

C. *Our Involvement in Redemption*
1. See John 17:18 and John 20:21
2. What is a soul worth? (Luke 9:24-25)
3. Our standard is pleasing God rather than simply avoiding violations in actual sin (2 Tim. 2:4).

4. Jesus our Grand Exemplar
   Follow Me—simple, but costly

The Silences of God

TEXT: John 14:1-2

Let not your heart be troubled: ye believe in God, believe also in me. In my Father's house are many mansions: if it were not so, I would have told you. I go to prepare a place for you.

A. *God Frequently Provides in Silence*
   1. The Son was promised long before He came. The seed of the woman was to bruise Satan's head (Gen. 3:15).
   2. The Son arrived "when the fulness of time was come" (Gal. 4:4).
B. *The Son Victorious—Even Before the Cross*
   1. No inner appeal toward Satan (John 14:30)
   2. Resurrection inevitable
      a. We are slow to believe—like two on Emmaus Road (Luke 24:13-32).
      b. It was not possible that the grave should hold Him (Acts 2:24).
      c. All the answers here provided for in our redemption.
C. *God's Basic Intentions for Us Are Good*
   1. In the Gift of His Son—will He not with Him also give us all things? (Rom. 8:32).
   2. Who is he that can harm you if you are zealous for what is right? (1 Pet. 3:13).
      Joseph—discovered God's intentions for good, after many years (Gen. 50:20).
   3. Our basic assignment is to trust Him always. We are safer than we think when we live in the will of God.

Entire Sanctification: A Second Crisis

TEXT: John 17:17

Sanctify them through thy truth: thy word is truth.

Introduction:
1. The truth equals the total gospel message
   a. Grounded in Calvary
   b. Affords us deliverance
   c. Affords us perspective
      (1) Allows for growth
      (2) Does not eliminate mistakes and blunders

A. *Some Fundamentals:*
   1. Truth the instrumental cause of our sanctification (entire).
   2. The Cross and His shed blood on Calvary affords us the meritorious cause for our sanctification, as well as our initial salvation (Heb. 13:12, RSV, Phillips).
   3. The Holy Spirit the efficient cause of our sanctification.

B. *This Truth Grounded in the Warp and Woof of the Total Biblical Revelation, Especially in the New Testament.*
   1. John the Baptist foretold (Matt: 3:11-12, RSV, Phillips)
   2. Jesus pictured this work in the symbol of water (John 7:37-39, RSV, Phillips, Wesley).
   3. Peter declared it on the day of Pentecost (Acts 2: 38-39, NIV, RSV).
   4. Peter reported that Gentiles also received this experience, some years after Pentecost (Acts 15: 8-9, Phillips, RSV).
   5. Paul outlined in his divine commission (Acts 26: 18, Phillips, RSV).
   6. Paul prayed for new Christians recently turned from heathenism (1 Thess. 5:23-24, NIV, NEB).

C. *The Prime (and Immediate) Condition Is Faith*
1. In His Word
   a. Wesley: "The commands of God are only covered promises"
   b. Present tense—now
      D. Steele: "The Holy Spirit for me now!"
2. Total commitment a condition of faith
   a. Based on merit of Calvary (Rom. 12:1-2, Wesley, Phillips)
   b. Faith the proper response to mercy

Our Presuppositions Versus God's Redemptive Plan

TEXT: John 20:15

Jesus saith unto her, Woman, why weepest thou? whom seekest thou? She, supposing him to be the gardener, saith unto him, Sir, if thou have borne him hence, tell me where thou hast laid him, and I will take him away.

Introduction:
1. Mary of Magdala, one of Jesus' most devoted followers
   a. See John 11:32-36
   b. See John 12:1-8, the anointing in advance for Jesus' coming death and burial.
2. Late at the tomb when Jesus was buried (Matt. 27:61)

A. *Sorrow and Love Brought Her Early*
1. The shock of the empty tomb (John 20:1)
   a. Theft seemed inevitable to her—done by enemies
   b. Jewish reverence for human body—even at death
      (1) No mutilation allowed

       (2) Brought forth Joseph of Arimathaea who gave his own tomb for Jesus.

       (3) Nicodemus also identified (furnished 75 lbs. of spices)

       (4) Women also prepared mixture of spices

  2. Mary had run for help to Peter and John

    a. John 20:2-9

    b. She stayed at the tomb after men left (v. 11).

B. *Beginning of Revelation*

  1. Her first look into tomb (vv. 11-12)

    a. Saw two angels in white

    b. Their question concerning her sobbing

C. *A Man Appears*

  1. Looked like the gardener

    a. Ordinary clothes?

      (1) Only God had humility enough for such a revelation

      (2) How often we try to outguess God!

    b. The Man's two searching questions:

      (1) Why weep?

      (2) Whom do you seek?

  2. Mary's dilemma

    a. Sought a corpse—out of love and memories

    b. What if God had granted her request?

      C. H. Lenski in *The Interpretation of St. John's Gospel:* "Indeed, why does she weep? —when we should all have had cause to weep to all eternity if what she wept for had been given her, the deady body of her Lord!"

    c. Have you ever prayed: "O God, edit my prayers; give me the desires of my heart rather than my asking petitions"?

D. *A Voice Is Heard*

  1. God is no Tantalus—to torment us—but He surprises us with better than our petitions.

  2. This devoted woman was the first to see and hear for herself.

3. The tone reveals the Person. "Mary!"
    a. Her confession, in Aramaic, "Rabonni!"—or Teacher, Master!
    b. A new order and a wider relationship through the Holy Spirit. ("Do not cling to Me" now.)
4. Her witness to the disciples
    a. "I have seen the Lord." ("She told them that he had said these things to her" [20:18].)
    b. Incredulous men (Luke 24:22-24)
5. He appears to the disciples twice
    a. John 20:19-29
    b. His marks remained
    c. Truth vindicated

Reference Notes

Introduction

1. J. H. Mayfield, "The Gospel According to John," *Beacon Bible Commentary* (Kansas City: Beacon Hill Press of Kansas City, 1965), 7:21.

2. R. H. Lightfoot, *St. John's Gospel: A Commentary,* C. F. Evans, ed. (New York: Oxford University Press, 1960), p. 1.

3. H. H. Hobbs, "An Exposition of the Gospel of John," *Exposition of the Four Gospels* (Grand Rapids: Baker Book House, 1968), p. 10.

4. James M. Boice, *The Gospel of John* (Grand Rapids: Zondervan Publishing House, 1969), 1:15.

5. *Ibid.,* p. 16.

Prologue

1. G. C. Morgan, *The Gospel According to John* (New York: Fleming H. Revell, Co., n.d.), p. 18.

2. B. F. Westcott, *The Gospel According to St. John* (Grand Rapids: William B. Eerdmans Publishing Co., 1950), 1:2.

3. Morgan, *John,* p. 25.

4. J. H. Jowett, *My Daily Meditation* (LaVerne, Calif.: El Camino Press, 1975), p. 187.

5. Boice, *John,* 1:35.

6. William Temple, *Readings in St. John's Gospel* (London: The Macmillan Co., 1939), p. 14.

First Year of Ministry

1. Temple, *Readings,* p. 24.

2. Alan Richardson, "The Gospel According to Saint John," *The Torch Bible Commentary* (London: SCM Press, Ltd., 1959), p. 156.

3. Jowett, *Daily Meditation,* p. 192.

4. Mayfield, "John," *BBC,* 7:42.

5. D. A. Redding, *The Miracles of Christ* (Westwood, N.J.: Fleming H. Revell Co., 1964), p. 4.

6. John Wesley, *The Works of John Wesley* (Naperville, Ill.: A. R. Allenson, Inc., Reprint 1958), 5:296.

7. Lightfoot, *St. John's Gospel,* pp. 65-66.

8. Morgan, *John,* p. 55.

9. Paul Scherer, *The Word God Sent* (New York: Harper and Row, 1965), p. 254.

10. Morgan, *John,* p. 59.

11. Leon Morris, "The Gospel According to John," *New International Commentary of the New Testament* (Grand Rapids: William B. Eerdmans Publishing Co., 1971), *loc. cit.*

12. Morgan, *John,* pp. 63-64.

13. *Ibid.,* p. 68.

14. *Ibid.,* p. 69.

15. Jowett, *Daily Meditation,* p. 220.

16. Roy L. Smith, *New Lights from Old Lamps* (New York: Abingdon-Cokesbury Press, 1953), p. 177.

17. Morgan, *John,* p. 17.

CENTRAL PERIOD OF MINISTRY

1. R. F. Bailey, quoted in Morris, "John," *NICNT,* pp. 346-47.

2. Temple, *Readings,* p. 88.

3. G. H. C. MacGregor, quoted in Morris, "John," *NICNT,* p. 362, fn. 81.

4. John Calvin, "The Gospel According to John," *Calvin's New Testament Commentaries* (Richmond, Va.: John Knox Press, 1960), p. 393, fn. 2.

5. Morgan, *John,* p. 149.

6. Jowett, *Daily Meditation,* p. 180.

7. Augustine, quoted in Morris, "John," *NICNT,* p. 483, fn. 46.

8. Chrysostom, quoted in *ibid.,* p. 494, fn. 46.

9. Jowett, *Daily Meditation.*

10. Morgan, *John,* p. 170.

11. William Barclay, *Jesus as They Saw Him* (New York: Harper and Row, 1962), p. 199.

12. Morris, "John," *NICNT,* p. 516.

13. Redding, *Miracles of Christ,* p. 149.

14. Calvin, "John," *CNTC,* p. 442.

15. *Ibid.,* p. 443.

The Shadows Lengthen

1. Morgan, *John,* pp. 208-9.

2. Temple, *Readings,* p. 196.

3. Morris, "John," *NICNT,* p. 592.

4. *Ibid.,* p. 609.

Final Discourses and Events

1. G. H. C. MacGregor, *The Gospel of John* (New York: Harper and Bros., 1928), p. 275.

2. Richardson, "John" *TBC,* p. 156.

3. William Barclay, "The Gospel According to St. John," *The Interpreter's Bible* (New York: Abingdon-Cokesbury Press, 1952), 2:185.

4. John Wesley, *Explanatory Notes upon the New Testament* (Naperville, Ill.: A. R. Allenson, Inc., reprint 1958), p. 370.

5. Temple, *Readings,* p. 240.

6. Lightfoot, *St. John's Gospel,* pp. 276-77.

7. G. C. Morgan, *The Westminster Pulpit,* (Westwood, N.J.: Fleming H. Revell Co., 1954), 1:223.

8. Morgan, *John,* p. 255.

9. C. W. Quinby, quoted in Hobbs, "John," *EFG,* p. 230.

10. Temple, *Readings,* pp. 271-72.

11. J. C. Ryle, quoted in Morris, "John," *NICNT,* p. 697, fn. 47.

12. *Ibid.,* p. 693.

13. Morgan, *Westminster Pulpit,* 1:153.

14. *Ibid.,* p. 161.

15. C. K. Barrett, *The Gospel According to St. John* (London: SPCK, 1955), p. 407.

16. Morris, "John," *NICNT*, p. 701.

17. *Ibid.*, p. 705.

18. John Calvin, quoted in *ibid.*

19. Lightfoot, *St. John's Gospel*, p. 294.

20. Morris, "John," *NICNT*, p. 713.

21. C. H. Dodd, *The Interpretation of the Fourth Gospel* (Cambridge: The University Press, 1953), p. 416, fn. 1.

22. Temple, *Readings*, p. 316.

23. Milligan and Moulton, quoted in Morris, "John," *NICNT*, p. 716.

24. Temple, *Readings*, pp. 312-13.

25. Walter Luthi, *St. John's Gospel* (Exposition), trans. (Richmond, Va.: John Knox Press, 1960), p. 259.

26. Edwyn C. Hoskyns, *The Fourth Gospel*, F. N. Davey, ed. (London: Faber and Faber, 1947), p. 495.

27. *Ibid.*, p. 504.

28. Luthi, *St. John's Gospel*, p. 260.

JESUS' ARREST, TRIAL, AND EXECUTION

1. Calvin, "John," *CNTC*, 2:195.

2. Redding, *Miracles of Christ*, p. 105.

3. Augustine, quoted in Morris, "John," *NICNT*, p. 757, fn. 49.

4. Chrysostom, quoted in *ibid.*, p. 751, fn. 29.

5. Barclay, *Jesus as They Saw Him*, p. 270.

6. Morgan, *John*, p. 284.

7. *Ibid.*, p. 295.

8. Morris, "John," *NICNT*, p. 818.

THE RESURRECTION

1. Temple, *Readings*, p. 375.

2. *Ibid.*

3. Lightfoot, *St. John's Gospel*, p. 330.

4. *Ibid.*, p. 332.

5. *Ibid.*

6. Hoskyns, *Fourth Gospel*, p. 540.

7. R. C. H. Lenski, "The Interpretation of St. John's Gospel," *Interpretation of the New Testament* (Columbus, Ohio: Lutheran Book Concern, 1942), p. 1351.

8. Temple, *Readings*, p. 383.

9. Hoskyns, *Fourth Gospel*, p. 547.

10. Morris, "John," *NICNT*, p. 846.

11. *Ibid.*, p. 848.

12. Barclay, *Jesus as They Saw Him*, p. 419.

13. Morgan, *John*, p. 323.

14. Morris, "John," *NICNT*, p. 856.

Selected Bibliography

I. Commentaries and Expositions

Barclay, William. "The Gospel According to St. John," *The Interpreter's Bible,* Vols. I and II. New York: Abingdon-don-Cokesbury Press, 1952.

Barrett, C. K. *The Gospel According to St. John.* London: SPCK, 1955.

Boice, James M. *The Gospel of John,* Vol. I (John 1:1—4:54) Grand Rapids: Zondervan Publishing House, 1969.

Calvin, John. "The Gospel According to John," *Calvin's New Testament Commentaries,* 12 vols. Translated by T. H. Parker. Grand Rapids: William B. Eerdmans Publishing Co., 1949.

Dood, C. H. *The Interpretation of the Fourth Gospel.* Cambridge: The University Press, 1953.

Gossip, A. J. "The Gospel According to St. John" (Exposition), *The Interpreter's Bible.* New York: Abingdon-Cokesbury Press, 1952.

Hobbs, H. H. "An Exposition of the Gospel of John," *Exposition of the Four Gospels.* Grand Rapids: Baker Book House, 1968.

Hoskyns, Edwyn C. *The Fourth Gospel.* Edited by F. N. Davey. London: Faber and Faber, 1947.

Lightfoot, R. H. *St. John's Gospel: A Commentary.* Edited by C. F. Evans. New York: Oxford University Press, 1960.

Lenski, R. C. H. "The Interpretation of St. John's Gospel," *Interpretation of the New Testament.* Columbus, Ohio: Lutheran Book Concern, 1942.

Luthi, Walter. *St. John's Gospel* (Exposition). Translated. Richmond, Va.: John Knox Press, 1960.

MacGregor, G. H. C. *The Gospel of John.* New York: Harper and Bros., 1928.

Mayfield, J. H. "The Gospel According to John," *Beacon Bible Commentary,* Vol. 7. Kansas City: Beacon Hill Press of Kansas City, 1965.

Morgan, G. C. *The Gospel According to John.* New York: Fleming H. Revell Co., n.d.

Morris, Leon. "The Gospel According to John," *New International Commentary of the New Testament.* Grand Rapids: William B. Eerdmans Publishing Co., 1971.

Quinby, C. W. *John, the Universal Gospel.* New York: The Macmillan Co., 1947.

Richardson, Alan. "The Gospel According to Saint John," *The Torch Bible Commentary.* London: SCM Press, Ltd., 1959.

Temple, William. *Readings in St. John's Gospel.* London: The Macmillan Co., 1939.

Tenney, M. C. *John: the Gospel of Belief.* Grand Rapids: William B. Eerdmans Publishing Co., 1948.

Westcott, B. F. *The Gospel According to St. John,* 2 vols. Grand Rapids: William B. Eerdmans Publishing Co., 1950.

Wesley, John. *Explanatory Notes upon the New Testament.* Naperville, Ill.: A. R. Allenson, Inc., Reprint 1958.

II. OTHER BOOKS *(involved in References and Notes)*

Barclay, William. *Jesus as They Saw Him.* New York: Harper and Row, 1962.

Jowett, J. H. *My Daily Meditation.* LaVerne, Calif.: El Camino Press, 1975.

Morgan, G. C. *The Westminster Pulpit.* 10 vols. Westwood, N.J.: Fleming H. Revell Co., 1954.

Redding, D. A. *The Miracles of Christ.* Westwood, N.J.: Fleming H. Revell Co., 1964.

Robertson, A. T. *Epochs in the Life of the Apostle John.* Grand Rapids: Baker Book House, 1976.

Scherer, Paul. *The Word God Sent.* New York: Harper and Row, 1965.

Smith, Roy L. *New Lights from Old Lamps.* New York: Abingdon-Cokesbury Press, 1953.

Sparks, H. F. D. *Johannine Synopsis of the Gospels.* New York: Harper and Row, 1974.

Wesley, John. *The Works of John Wesley,* Vol. V. Kansas City: Nazarene Publishing House, n.d.

AUTHOR

Young, Samuel

TITLE

Beacon Bible Expositi

DATE DUE	BORROWER'S NA